THE YEARS OF
Travelling Anxiously

THE YEARS OF *Travelling Anxiously*

A Travel Writer's Search for Peace of Mind

TOM SYKES

ICON

Published in the UK in 2026 by
Icon Books Ltd, Omnibus Business Centre,
39–41 North Road, London N7 9DP
email: info@iconbooks.com
www.iconbooks.com

ISBN: 978-183773-255-5
eBook: 978-183773-256-2

Typeset by SJmagic DESIGN SERVICES, India

Printed and bound in the UK

Appointed GPSR EU Representative: Easy Access System Europe Oü, 16879218
Address: Mustamäe tee 50, 10621, Tallinn, Estonia
Contact Details: gpsr.requests@easproject.com, +358 40 500 3575

For Amara, who's done more than anyone else to make this anxious traveller less anxious – and you don't even know it yet.

CONTENTS

INTRODUCTION

WHAT WE DON'T KNOW WE KNOW ABOUT ANXIOUS TRAVEL

1

I thought I'd learned. Grown. Don't we all? We cling to these stories of progress in both society and our personal lives. From birth we're fed maxims about life getting easier as it goes. Face your fear, conquer your fear. 'That which does not kill us, makes us stronger,' wrote Nietzsche. I thought I'd spent enough time in the Philippines to have squished all fear of it. After living here plus eight trips over the last thirteen years, I've toughed out the heat, the traffic jams, the pollution, two minor car crashes. I've been to the places where drug-users were executed by vigilantes. I've interviewed an activist who was hounded at home by a soldier who warned them to stop dissing the regime – or die. I stayed cool on all those occasions.

I thought I'd devised strategies. I'd learned to pass the auto-stalemates by looking out the window and noting graffiti, adverts or the arbitrary poetry of urban breakdown – storm-dislodged hyacinths mantling the Pasig River, kids racing each other through a concrete pipe abandoned diagonally across a Cubao backstreet. If there was nothing to see, I'd read a book or pen my own. Writers shouldn't be short of material in a mesmerising city like Manila.

So why now am I in a taxi on Kalayaan Avenue, Quezon City, shaking like machine gun recoil, battling for my breath, launching water down my torrid throat? Why has the soothing inner voice of curiosity – *how interesting is this, how fascinating is that* – declined into the gravelly tones of paranoia? *Will I make my interview on time? Are my questions facile and white and privileged? Do I smell? Why is the hand-fan strapped to the head rest in front of me only multiplying the amount of warm air rather than cooling me down? Will I have enough change for the driver at drop-off? Does the driver know where he's going? Am I going to die? A Philippine taxi with rear seatbelts is as common as a good film starring Gerard Butler.*

These are rookie worries – or should be. Worrying about these worries only adds to the worry. It's a self-perpetuating process. Distraction is needed. Breathe in through the nose, out through the mouth. That's the advice. Easier said than done when a main symptom of my anxiety is imagining I can't breathe. But how imagined is it? I've been failing to quit smoking for a decade – I could have damaged my lungs. Mental and physical health are wedded, they say. That doesn't make me feel better.

What *does* work is beer. But it's 9.22am and that's not an option ... yet. I could warrant one at lunchtime with my interviewees. They'll see me gulp San Miguel and barely eat ... until I've drunk enough to stop freaking out about choking on food. That's another symptom. My interviewees shouldn't judge – they know the Western weakness for the sauce. If they do judge, I'll take the risk. I'll also risk feeling worse tomorrow from a hangover. But when anxious I can only aim for short-term relief. I never learn.

2

I've had many crises like this in my years of travelling anxiously. I spent most of that trip to the Philippines in a state of agitation. It's a medically defined acute form of restlessness that compels you to fidget and generally keep moving your body. It was first recorded as a side effect of anxiety by the ancient Greek physician Hippocrates, who made reference to 'trembling'. In the eighteenth century, European doctors would diagnose agitation in those suffering from the 'vapours' or 'nervousness'. During that fateful time in Manila, if I stayed still my heart rate would surge and challenge glabrous-headed techno-nerd Moby for his Guinness World Record for the track with the fastest bpm (1,000, as it happens, and the tune is called 'Thousand', appropriately). Into the symptom mix can go head-spinning nausea, the sensation that slow-setting concrete has been shovelled into my lungs and a veritable Niagara of perspiration. Unfortunately, my sweat cleaves to my backside, leaving embarrassing stains. More embarrassingly, the agitation that hit me while attending an academic conference made me get up periodically and saunter to the other end of a seminar room. This put off the poor junior researcher who was delivering their first public talk – and nervous enough themselves. And of course, my embarrassment about embarrassing them only fed the anxiety beast.

Rationally speaking, there was nothing disturbing about that conference. I'd spoken at many before and I'd been looking forward to this one. But panic isn't rational, by definition. I just about held it together until the end-of-event drinks reception. An underhand move my anxiety makes is convincing me that the latest crisis is not mental but entirely physical – a bug, a stroke, a coronary. This self-deceit will make me do something that will trouble others and thus bring further shame to me. In this instance, I had symptoms that were new to me, including severe indigestion, which told me that this wasn't the usual drill and required medical help.

The conference convenor called me an ambulance. It pulled up outside the conference hall astonishingly fast for Manila, a city of petrified traffic. I lay on a stretcher, had devices stuck on me. My blood pressure and heart rate were stratospheric. While a tiny island of sense-making still left in my fear-flooded head told me these were the typical signs of a panic attack, the rising levels of paranoia told me they were the *causes* of it. Chicken and egg. While I was strapped up and wheeled off, colleagues looked on in startled pity, wine glasses in hand. *Do they think I'm a lunatic being dragged off to the asylum? That I have a contagious disease they're now at risk of? If this turns out to be a fear-episode – which it likely will – should I feel guilty about wasting the time and money of the beleaguered Philippine health system? Will someone else with a 'proper' illness die because my histrionics deprived them of medical attention?*

3

While I couldn't work out what had ailed me on that trip, I returned from the Philippines hoping to have left behind whatever it was. I was foolish to believe that. Summer 2018 was exceedingly rough. I averted a breakdown through a middle-class combination of sea-swimming and meditation. In one meditation I had an epiphany. After feeling the tranquility that's the goal of this enterprise, an intense sadness came over me. I wept and wept, the face of my close friend Gareth, who'd died four months ago, shimmering in my mind's eye.

Later I came across a theory that anxiety is the nasty dividend of failing to express emotions, especially grief. It's like a beer pipe in a pub that doesn't get cleaned. Dirt builds up to the stage that a pint pulled through that pipe will upset a punter's stomach. I hadn't done the necessary spiritual 'cleaning' work. I hadn't allowed myself to grieve for Gareth just after his death. I'd bottled my grief up – to continue the boozing metaphor – and tried to abandon it by travelling 6,500 miles to the Philippines. I've since learned that geographical distance and psychological distance are different things. In fact, travelling physically away from a problem of the mind or soul can bring you closer to it, emotionally speaking. In Thomas Mann's 1925 novel *The Magic Mountain*, young Hans Castorp feels that he's leaving 'home and regular living' behind as his train makes the steep ascent into the Swiss Alps. But escaping to a sanatorium in a placid landscape away from the hubbub of civilisation only amplifies his fears and doubts about illness, life and love. My fate was less ambiguous than Hans', though. (If you don't know what I mean by this I'm not going to spoil the plot of that novel here.) My grief, undealt with at the time, was allowed to fester and mutate into almost 24/7 distress for three months.

For many, anxiety is triggered by current or coming events. The hot flush as you wait to be called for the interview. The arrhythmia attending the driving test. The bubbling belly before you deliver the public pronouncement. I've been that guy – I still am sometimes. I'm not proud to share this, but I once prayed to whatever might be out there to make the public building I was in fall down. Inside this building, I was about to read out some of my writing to a crowd of eleven. I was in such a psychic mess that I would have preferred crushing twenty people – including me – to death than have to stand up and speak some words into a microphone.

It sounds ridiculous when you strip down an experience like that to its bare elements. Reactionaries, 'anti-woke' crusaders and just general arseholes will claim that nothing anyone does today is as anxiety-inducing as going over the top in the First World War. But that misses several points. Anxiety is culturally and historically relative – if you pulled a Tommy out of the trenches and whisked him in a time machine to twenty-first-century Britain, he might have a meltdown trying to use Instagram or accepting that Liz Truss was ever allowed near the levers of British power. Secondly, as mentioned, the dread felt before or during an activity often has nothing to do with said activity.

4

If anxious feelings always were directly related to the task at hand, I'd have been convinced I was dying while being harassed by bellicose beggars at the Ghana–Côte d'Ivoire border, rather than suddenly feeling that way while drinking a cup of tea one Sunday morning in my home in the south of England. I still can't fathom how the latter event could lead to abject terror for two hours ... which led to another ambulance call. But at least, when the ambulance does come, and the kit is wheeled out, and the paramedics assure me I'm not going to die – 'If you were eighty, mate, I might be worried, but you're forty, so I'm not' – the freak-out halts. I'm reassured that, if this isn't a panic attack and it's something that could kill me, I have the best people here to stop me getting killed. It's the opposite of what they call white coat syndrome. Although these NHS workers are employed – for not enough respect or money – as physical healers, the aid they've given me is closer to what a shrink or shaman dispenses.

At other times, when my life's been in genuine peril, I've settled into a strangely blank state of mind. I've been at risk of drowning twice – both times off beaches in Southeast Asia – and evolution intercepted panic. Some survival instinct dulled my fear, took possession of my limbs and propelled me like some clockwork toy against the overbearing current back to the safety of the shore.

If the anguish on my last trip to Manila was traceable to grief over my friend, what's the current consternation about? I can't think of a spiritual knockback of late. So, what if my anxiety is the sign of a deeper, trickier malaise? In sort-of-Freudian mode, anxiety can stem from an unconscious conflict. But what one? This is a big question. It requires investigation. I feel like a sleuth of the soul, a Philip Marlowe of my own mental health. How do I find out if the malaise is professional in nature? Existential? Emotional? Intellectual? A sickly cocktail of all the above? Perhaps I'm not being authentic. Perhaps everyone frets about that in our age of surface and imitation. Over the course of my life, I might have been lying to others and to myself. Maybe everyone does that, too. Am I playing at being the cocky, Hemingwayesque foreign reporter? The macho geezer who boasts over whiskies at the bar about weathering the hurricanes – literally or otherwise – of the Global South? I don't do this consciously, but then it's what goes on in the unconscious that really matters, many would argue. But I must have made a conscious decision to use the argot of war at the start of this book – all that talk of 'battling' and 'machine gun recoil'. That's not me. I don't know what a machine gun sounds or looks like outside of the movies. I've never had a fight in my life. I'm not that kind of man.

5

You can drive yourself mad – or more anxious – by trying to second guess what that deeper malaise is, what's *really* making you anxious, what you *don't know* you know is bringing the pain. In Nigeria during the run-up to my wedding, I was struggling with what I call low-level anxiety. Much more on this later. Low-level anxiety is manageable – for me – with beer, which keeps the mood just buoyant enough to avoid paralysis. On that trip I tried to convince myself that I didn't need to be anxious since I was, on paper, having the time of my life. I was travelling in my beloved West Africa, learning about animism (more on this later, too), listening to great music, eating great food, getting to know my imminent in-laws and, above all, marrying the woman I loved – and still love – more than anyone in the world.

So why the fear? Was it a flare fired from the icy waters of my unconscious up into the clouds of my conscious to tell me that I was about to make some dire existential mistake? Was it the psychical equivalent of a wedding guest throwing up their hand when the vicar pops the question: 'Does anyone know of any lawful impediment to this marriage?' And then naturally my thoughts turned to how to suppress the anxiety, what size of bone to throw to this particular Rottweiler-of-the-soul to stop it snarling. If unbeknownst to my conscious mind I didn't want to marry Oge and this anxiety was a result of denying it, would calling the whole thing off be the best option?

6

What I'm plagued by now, here in Manila, is also low-level anxiety. I don't rule out graduating to something worse. As this taxi ride drags on, I ponder what the current heebie-jeebies are code for, what they're trying to tell me, if anything. All I can think of is an ongoing obsession with my health. This isn't the kind of health obsession that has resulted in my being healthy, I hasten to add. On the contrary – the demons and the angels of my nature are fighting it out, and the demons are winning. I'm way more susceptible to the id, which tempts me to smoke and drink and eat junk, rather than the superego, which politely advises doing pilates and munching kale. For a Westerner in Manila there are myriad temptations to be unhealthy. I tend to associate my downtimes here with partying. But I was 30 when I was living here. In those halcyon days I could get away with chain smoking Marlboros and guzzling San Miguel. Now, aged 43, I'm overweight, on meds for gout and blood pressure and … well there's nothing more tedious than a list of someone's medical problems. In short, I can't get away with it anymore.

Inevitably, dwelling on this only ups the anxiety. I opt for different relief that's healthier than beer: I play a game on my phone. Contrary to the folk devil image of video games turning our kids into maudlin ghouls, they can boost our wellbeing, too. Psychologist Christian M. Jones and colleagues concluded that games can generate 'positive emotions', 'contribute to emotional stability', reduce 'emotional disturbances in children' and serve as 'a means of stress relaxation and stress reduction'. Just now, I'm gaining respite from taking everything too seriously by concentrating on an unserious text adventure based on a science fiction 'gamebook' I loved as a kid. Nostalgia is part of the appeal and it puts me into a happier headspace. Unfortunately, distraction doesn't always come easily to me.

7

I must get through the next fortnight in Manila, somehow. I'll do the necessary to survive in the short run, as I've done on every anxiety-clouded trip I've made, not only to the Philippines and Nigeria, but to France, Côte d'Ivoire, India, Nepal and elsewhere. But more challenging have been the longer-term causes and consequences of my travel fear. Addressing them has been a motive to write this book.

It's important to say that I haven't endured the same degree of stress as travellers like war correspondents or military personnel. Some of their experiences are shared in this book, but this story is mainly about my struggles with what many would consider 'easier' journeys, that are objectively closer to those that most people take for work or pleasure. Whereas the dread that strikes the soldier, for instance, can be traced back to the trauma of witnessing death, the dread dogging those of us who do fairly ordinary things on the road can be harder to figure out.

Anxiety is also hard to define because its symptoms and effects vary. The *Oxford English Dictionary* describes 'anxious' quite broadly: '1. Experiencing worry, nervousness, or unease; 2. very eager and concerned to do something or for something to happen.' In their eye-opening little book *Anxiety: A Very Short Introduction*, Daniel Freeman and Jason Freeman dub anxiety an 'emotion'. At the same time, they say that it can be 'a pretty mysterious experience' and quote Holly Golightly, the protagonist of Truman Capote's novel *Breakfast at Tiffany's*, whose 'mean reds' encapsulated emotions, thoughts and physical sensations, that were in contrast to the better-known 'blues': 'You're afraid and you sweat like hell, but you don't know what you're afraid of. Except something bad is going to happen, only you don't know what it is.'

Other writers have weighed in with their definitions. Marcel Proust's novels throb with unease about the fleeting nature of existence, how the march of time tramples over events and people important to us, reducing them to blurred or unreliable memories. Proust's characters are often trammelled by status anxiety, fretting as to whether they are self-confident and well-bred enough for class-obsessed France in the 1910s. For Mrs Dalloway, the creation of that other modernist maestro Virginia Woolf, the burden of conforming to 1920s values leads to angst about mortality and meaninglessness. Mrs D's psychological 'double', Septimus Smith, is beset by similar social pressures as well as PTSD from his terrifying time in the trenches. The admixture has the effect of vinegar cut with bicarbonate of soda – his anxiety bubbles over, can't be suppressed and he takes his own life.

In the menacing yarns of Woolf's contemporary Franz Kafka, individuals are tormented by impersonal bureaucracies that they can neither understand nor appease. The universe is no friendlier, its absurdities and random cruelties offering little for humans to hope or trust in. The poor bloke who transforms into an insect in *Metamorphosis* is a metaphor for our estrangement from both society and our own identities.

Jean-Paul Sartre thought that anxiety – he preferred the term 'anguish' – arose from the realisation that we are all free individuals who can make our own choices and create our own meanings. This might sound like a privilege until you realise that it means taking absolute responsibility for yourself and your behaviour and not relying on previous philosophies or ideologies as a guide. This doesn't mean we can act selfishly or in ways that hurt others, though. 'In fashioning myself, I fashion Man,' as Sartre put it.

The conflict reporter and filmmaker Iain Overton views his particular travel anxiety through Sartre's prism. The freedom to roam was alluring to the young Iain, but over his career has sparked 'nausea, disorientation and anxiety' on hairy trips to Somalia, Afghanistan, Iraq, Ukraine and other trouble spots.

'I've always wanted to go to places that haven't been captured by the digital footprint because therein lie stories that haven't been told from a journalistic perspective,' Iain told me. 'But where my younger self would have said, "Okay, there's nothing on this area so let's go," my older self has tended to fear going to places about which there's absolutely no information because the potential for horror is greater.'

A converse pattern of travel, where people from the poor Global South move to the rich Global North, can provoke anxiety. Postcolonial writers from Carlos Bulosan to Sam Selvon to Chimamanda Ngozie Adichi have explored the disquiet caused by discrimination, bigotry, job insecurity, loss of status, destruction of family ties and other predicaments faced by the immigrant outsider.

The numerous flavours of travel anxiety described in this book resonate with all these takes since travelling involves matters of time, memory, identity and human interaction, and can put you into conflict with authority and compel you to make choices that affect yourself and others.

An important disclaimer: I have no training in mental health and so will not offer expert analysis of it. Nor can or should I dispense clinical advice to anyone. For reasons that will become clearer as you read on, if you're looking to me as your guru then you must be in a very dark place indeed. Others *are* qualified to offer counsel, and I discuss them in this book because their theories and remedies make sense to me as an anxious traveller.

As a result of writing this book I've been able to answer some of the questions above about myself and my affliction, though not others. In the complex world of fear, trauma, consciousness and selfhood, some questions will never have straight answers, I'm afraid to say. My story is, like others', not a simple arc of improvement from anxious traveller to non-anxious traveller. On the journey there have been many delays, distractions, wrong turns and reversals. But the destination I've reached has at least given me a better understanding of my condition and contained some of its worst effects. So, if any of that is in any way helpful to other anxious travellers, or anyone who gets anxious about anything, well, I'll consider it an accomplishment.

PART 1. AGITATION IN MANILA

1

So here I am in Manila, in the back of the taxi, drenched in anxiety. Again. It's all so exasperatingly repetitive. The game on my phone isn't cutting it, and I fix on the probably ludicrous idea that the city itself is the source of my woes. In her hauntingly phantasmal novel *State of War*, the great Filipina author Ninotchka Rosca writes, 'the city came out of chaos, lived with chaos, and would survive any chaos. The question was... whether it could survive order and reason'. To what extent is chaos, then, in Manila's DNA? It seems to me that chaos – an absence of order or control – is closely related to anxiety, fear, panic. Do these traits make for a Manila Syndrome in the sense of the notorious Jerusalem Syndrome?

In that same city, Australian Denis Michael Rohan burned down the al-Aqsa Mosque and, upon arrest, claimed that God had told him to do it. It would smooth the Second Coming of Christ, he added. Briton Oliver McAfee hiked out of Jerusalem and vanished in the Negev desert, leaving a trail of pages ripped from the Bible relating Jesus' 40 days in the wilderness. An Irishwoman came to the city and grew convinced that she was pregnant with the baby Prince of Peace 2.0. She didn't disclose the identity of the father. On his visit, an American man started to believe that he was the reincarnation of Samson, the biblical proto-superhero. Another American rediscovered his evangelical faith in middle age, flew to Jerusalem and camped in the lobby of a budget hostel introducing himself to all-comers as the 'new Messiah'. Ever since the medieval pilgrimages, folks have been coming to Jerusalem and succumbing to spiritual delusions. In the 1980s and 90s, reported cases of Jerusalem Syndrome peaked at 100 a year, a total of 40 lost souls needing treatment in a psychiatric unit.

In his penetrating book *Places of the Heart*, psychologist Colin Ellard shows that modern city-dwellers are driven spare by social inequality, lack of 'neighbourhood cohesion' and 'the possibility of exposure to toxins or pathogens'. Nothing new here – the poet William Wordsworth was in the late 1700s blaming loneliness, suspicion, jealousy, oneupmanship and ignorance on the crowded, polluted, turbo-paced cities of the industrial revolution. More scientifically, Ellard has found evidence that urban features can sabotage our state of mind. In a city like Jerusalem, you're besieged by so much religious architecture, activity, symbolism and history. This, coupled with the shock that many of us receive when we travel anywhere radically different, could ignite a psychotic episode.

Jerusalem isn't the only city with its own syndrome. Since the 1980s, Japanese tourists in Paris have reported paranoia, identity crisis and full-blown hallucinations resulting from language barriers, shock at the serene French temperament and displeasure that the real Paris fell short of the image they were expecting from brochures and magazines. In 2006, rumours emerged that the Japanese embassy in the City of Love had set up a round-the-clock phone line for anyone nobbled by Paris Syndrome. Embassy staff denied its existence, though.

Similar symptoms show in cases of Stendhal Syndrome, even if the apparent cause – glimpsing beautiful works of art in Florence – seems like a nice problem to have. The French novelist Stendhal was probably the first victim, complaining in 1817 after viewing the Basilica de Santa Croce, 'I had palpitations of the heart, what in Berlin they call "nerves". Life was drained from me. I walked with the fear of falling.'

My taxi jerks to a stop in a part of Quezon City that is no work of art. Its planners must have scoured Ellard's book for all the things *not to do* when designing an urban milieu. My trembling hands drop some banknotes in the driver's lap and fling open the door. The burst of hot air knocks the wind out of me. I pant and scan my surrounds. I'm in what Ellard would call a 'stress-point': a street market squatting against the rampart of a shopping mall, coagulated with noise, objects and bodies. There's no empty space between the vast decks of duck eggs, lime-like *calamansi* fruit sprinkled on black tarpaulins, flies riding the backs of smoked *bangus* fishes arranged sprucely on banana leaves, carts overflowing with an unruly jungle of blade-like chilli and *sambong* leaves, the summits of which are teetering with *durian* fruits and *taro*, root vegetables resembling old apothecary jars. Nor is there room between these wares and the customers and the vendors who have white scarves around their heads and wear long baggy shorts and sleeveless basketball jerseys. All the benches are occupied by topless, off-duty jeepney and tricycle drivers asleep with scraggy, greasy-furred cats and dogs at their feet or on the cracked paving below them. This slew of life forms existing at close quarters is another scourge of city life, according to Ellard. Our ancestors spent so long in small settlements, where everyone knew and trusted one another, that today we haven't yet evolved to handle bigger populations who are strangers to each other and constantly competing for money, work and attention. That's another recipe for place-anxiety – certainly from where I'm standing.

I feel ever more trapped. My freedom to move has been curtailed. I can't orient myself. 'It's difficult to see what's round the corner' and 'potential flight paths are blocked' – two further sources of place-anxiety in Ellard's book. The latter becomes literally true when I look over at the southern end of the road and the entrance to a side street that's obstructed by a precarious stack of goods – a sofa, a fridge, bookshelves, a TV. It's as if someone was in the middle of moving house only to have been gazumped at the eleventh hour.

My instincts now firmly in flight mode, I start towards some bushes across the road, nebulously maroon like dyed smoke used to mark targets in a Second World War film. I soon twig that these bushes are marooned from any kind of natural space that Ellard says can 'mitigate the risk of psychiatric disorders in urban populations'.

I turn back to the market and beseech any force out there that might make everything fucking alright.

Unsure how to access the mall, I skirt the perimeter of the market. I'm forced on to the busy road, since the pavement has been colonised by the sprawling market. Traffic is a prime trigger for what Ellard calls 'adrenaline baths', based on research he conducted on pedestrians in another Global Southern megacity, Mumbai. Like his subjects, I have to perform an 'intricate dance': sidestepping and leaning away from a speeding tricycle in an ungainly version of what characters do in 'bullet time' in the *Matrix* films. Ellard's subjects were seriously stressed, their blood pressure and 'sweat gland responses ... off the charts', the cortisol generated doing all flavours of harm. When Ellard interviewed these same people, they claimed to be unflustered by the maelstrom of heat, noise and traffic they withstood daily. Perhaps cultural norms forbade them to complain. If someone asks me right now how I feel about almost getting run down by oncoming vehicles, I'll probably burst into tears.

As I reach the northern frontier of the market, a monstrous high-rise hoves into view. It's been weathered and polluted into at least five shades of grey, its vertical lines of mansard roofs pearl-hued, its lower-down concrete panels almost charcoal. These are the Legaspi Towers 100, I find out later, and they're oppressively angular. The façade panels end abruptly above the main building, giving off a sharp, antenna-like vibe. I think of stabbing and impaling and the proverbial parental caution: 'you'll have your eye out with that'. I'm far from flabbergasted to find out that 'Jagged edges are hard, repulsive, and may signal risk,' in Ellard's view. On the other side of the equation, 'we have a near universal preference for curved contours', he writes. 'We see curves as soft, inviting, and beautiful.' I duly stop looking at this great big scary dagger in the sky.

The Legaspi Towers 100 are part of Manila's brutalist heritage, but lots of Manileños wish they weren't. Others wish there was no brutalist heritage in Manila at all. The towers were built in 1973 soon after President Marcos declared martial law. He wasn't the first dictator to cultivate a hypermasculine image and rule by terror. I'm not the first writer to observe that the Legaspi Towers 100 are not the only tall, phallic and daunting edifices built during this dismal phase of Philippine history.

Ellard argues that our mood can be affected by the shapes not only of buildings but of lettering and branding. Halfway between the towers and where I'm standing is a sign reading SOGO, the letters joined up like the Olympic rings. They're all curves and no corners, just as Ellard would like, and they're almost as common a sight around the Philippines as the golden arches of McDonald's. SOGO is a budget hotel chain, its success partly down to the easy-going shapeliness of its logo but also to the fact that rooms can be booked by the hour. Underneath this particular sign is a slogan that indicates where SOGO comes from: 'So clean ... so good.' In my twisted state, seeing a hotel advertise itself as 'so clean' only makes me picture the opposite: filthy bedclothes, broken toilets, cockroaches scuttling in sinks. I guess it's a variant on the social psychologist Daniel Wegner's 'white bear phenomenon': if someone tells you *not* to think of a white bear you will *inevitably* think of a pallid caniform of the Ursidae family.

By now I've no idea what I'm doing or where I'm going. It's pure luck that I find a palm-tree-bordered side entrance to the mall. The relief is like a fast-acting painkiller. I know it'll be short-lived, but short-lived is better than sod-all.

While I wait for a female security guard to stop twirling her baton and search my backpack at the entrance to the mall, I remind myself not to blame my anxiety on any one place. The story is more complex. While there's a popular belief – which has sold newspapers and seduced web traffic – that Jerusalem Syndrome besets those with no history of mental illness, the researchers Kalian and Witzum found that most victims had pre-existing conditions. The same is true of the other disorders I've mentioned. Like the bloke who leaves a 'happy marriage' behind in Darwin or Dagenham to turn sex pest in Bangkok or Busan, travel – plus white male privilege – can serve as excuses for behaviour unacceptable at home. At least five years before he torched that mosque in Jerusalem in 1969, Dennis Michael Rohan was hearing voices in his head. There were mosques in his native Australia at that time, so did he wait until going to Israel to commit his crime because he believed that that culture would be more sympathetic towards his demented desire to build heaven on Earth? If so, he must have had stereotypes in mind dodgier than a Diddy party.

Less destructively, there's a timeworn tradition of Westerners projecting their fear and loathing onto non-Western cities in a judgemental or, worse, racist manner. Just because I'm feeling the chaos of Manila that Rosca so vividly describes doesn't mean the chaos is Manila's fault. Indeed, in a postcolonial society like the Philippines, a lot of the chaos is the fault of people who look and sound like me. There's another reason to be uneasy. As Iain Overton says of his own travels to the Global South, 'I was conscious of my complicity in global warming and mass tourism. I was helping to bring wealth into those communities that I was filming but simultaneously I was eroding the cultural uniqueness of these locations. When I went back to some of these locations twenty years later I saw that now there was a Starbucks and facilities for the backpacker community. Everything was in English, and I'm not begrudging that – it means a new generation of people can go there. But I'd worry that we'd made everything familiar and accessible, which is a form of colonialism. I didn't realise I was doing it at the time. That brings some anxiety to my heart now.'

The other side of that coin is the many people from the non-West who come to the West and have an anxious time of it. Ann Bajo, now an academic but formerly a defence analyst with the Armed Forces of the Philippines, won her travel spurs surviving terrorist attacks in the southern Philippines and a school shooting in Manila in 2022. As a young woman of colour, she's had hard times on British streets. 'When I walk around Portsmouth or Liverpool,' she tells me, 'local guys will proposition me or make, shall we say, unsolicited comments. One time this man lifted his shirt up and yelled, "Do you want some of this, love?"

'In the Philippines, if something happens to me it's easy to shout, "Hey, help me here." I feel more vulnerable in the UK, as I don't think people will come to my aid. One of my professors told me that she was on a ferry on the Solent and saw a girl about to jump off the ferry, and nobody did anything about it. It was down to my professor to approach her and ask her, "Are you okay?"'

For Ann, that's a matter of cultural or behavioural difference between the West and the Philippines. In her home country 'there would have been security guards to help that girl. It's like people here in the UK are so individual and isolationist that they've forgotten that they belong to a community. It's weird. I'm not saying that everyone has to be smiling all the time but there's a lot of unfriendliness here.'

I try to count my lucky stars as a large white male who can look after himself in a place that is generally friendly towards large white males. It's a privilege I should check.

'This is me, not you,' I mutter to a concrete pillar that divides a make-your-own-bubble-tea station from a shop selling agricultural drones. I turn to catch a glower from a trouser-suited saleswoman leaning over a model condominium. But I don't care.

Go ahead and think I've lost my mind. You probably believe all white people are crazy or creepy anyway, based on the ones you see in Manila. And I can't fault that. My only aim is to get to my lunch date and not fuck that up.

2

I'm forever wowed by Philippine shopping malls. They have everything. Under late capitalism most human needs and wants can be satisfied within one building the size of a town. There are clinics, dental practices, chapels, tutoring services, ice skating rinks, oxygen bars, automated massage chairs, gunsmiths, aquariums, 'virtual girlfriend experiences', flight simulators, supermarkets and shops selling every other item thinkable. Any hunch I might have had that there are still limits to what can be bought and sold in these spaces disappears when a fiftysomething woman offers me a massage.

I mouth 'no' and keep walking. She follows.

'Sir, I think you travel a lot. You get tired easy. Massage for relaxation?'

'I'm in a rush, thank you.'

'There would be happy ending,' she says as blithely as someone else might share the weather forecast.

'I'm married,' I lie.

'To a Filipina or white?'

'Er, none of your business.'

The woman pinches the skin on her forearm. 'I am lighter, like white girl, see?'

'Really, no thanks.'

I realise I'm thirty minutes early for lunch. Another component of my travel anxiety is a phobia about being late. It's absurd in a culture where fashionable tardiness reigns and nobody hates you for being impeded by traffic or extreme weather. But, for me, this symptom merges horribly with the agitated urge to stay on the move, to reach the next destination in the hope it'll bring peace.

It never will. Humans desire what they lack but can't attain, says the psychoanalyst Todd McGowan. When people get what they think they want, they aren't satisfied. Consider the lengths someone can go to court the 'love of their life', only for the pair to get together and the relationship fall apart after months. How many actors and musicians achieve their dream of stardom only to overdose or commit suicide? Or what of the countless leaders across history who spiralled into corruption and murder because whatever power they gained was never ever enough?

For McGowan via the French theorist Jacques Lacan, what we really crave is the effort made to get what we think we want, which masochistically involves pain and torment.

This explains why stories in our culture focus on a quest rather than its resolution. Most of the running time of an action film shows a hero struggling for what they desire through fighting baddies, driving fast cars and flirting with an attractive co-star. Once the hero has accomplished their objectives, we might have five minutes of them being thanked by the mayor or snogging said co-star – and that's it. The journey, as it were, is much more meaningful than the destination.

Mark Manson, in his Gonzo self-help book *The Subtle Art of Not Giving a F*ck*, calls this the 'value of suffering'. We gain golden insights from failing and losing – insights like how to avoid failing and losing in the future. You can't achieve anything substantial without struggle. Manson writes of those who want to get rich but can't handle 'sixty-hour workweeks' and 'arbitrary corporate hierarchies', those in search of an 'amazing physique' who can't 'appreciate the pain and physical stress' of constant exercise, those jonesing for the perfect partner who won't put up with rejection and 'staring blankly at a phone that never rings.'

The value of suffering for a traveller-writer lies in finding material in the problems that arise on a trip. The hardiest of our species is the war reporter who's addicted to the adrenaline rush that accompanies every firefight and air strike. As the travel writer Shafik Meghji, who's been in harder scrapes than I have, says, 'When something dramatic or difficult happens, that's copy, right?' While researching his book *Crossed Off the Map* in the city of Cochabamba in Bolivia, he 'was out one evening and heard gunfire going off. I saw the protestors being "dispersed" by the police – people were running in all directions. Whatever plans I had for that day or for the next day, and indeed for that trip, would have to be curtailed.' But the incident was 'an anecdote that you can use as a writer – not to treat serious issues lightly, of course,' says Shafik. 'I was writing a book about Bolivia so that protest was a vivid example of what was going on socially and politically. I got a first-hand example of what it's like to be at a protest, or to be a student or campaigning about human rights issues at that moment.

'The key thing you're doing as a writer is giving people an accurate – at least from your perspective – account of a destination. That's not always positive. Lots of people will face hassles and difficulties and occasional dangers on their trips, and so if you can write about these from personal experience, it's beneficial, it's interesting, isn't it?'

Can't say I get it myself – what little violence I've encountered on my travels has repulsed me. As you've just seen, I can hardly cope with walking down a street in peacetime let alone one ripped apart by conflict. As far as my own struggle as a writer will yield literary dividends, frankly I'd trade in any further chance of such success for relief from the mental mayhem I'm embroiled in right now. But it doesn't work like that, for McGowan and Manson. The value of these scary and unpleasant experiences only arrives *after* they have happened, when they are recorded and crafted into a narrative, with however small a fee and bunch of people who will read it persuading the writer that it was worth going through hell after all.

3

I took the train from Portsmouth to Heathrow on a magnificently bright and still day. There was no risk of being delayed or deterred by the wacky weather swings that are typical of a small, cold, flood-prone island increasingly at the mercy of climate change. The train was punctual and reasonably priced despite aeons of neglect, underfunding and profiteering. Checking in at the airport was quick and simple, with no aggro caused by technical errors or authoritarian personalities. I sat in the business class lounge drinking cocktails and eating canapés. I was bored, of course, but this was a higher class of boredom than you get with a cheaper ticket. On the plane I had enough leg space, there were several films I wanted to see on the entertainment system and the food and drink was first-rate: steak; lobster thermidor; champagne; claret.

On my first day in Manila I did some sightseeing in Intramuros, the old Spanish town. I took nice pictures, ate nice food, bought nice presents for loved ones. On my second day I met my local contacts Jejo and Manny, had a nice lunch with them, and got some useful information for a new research network I'm building between British and Filipino academics. On my third day I visited a major university, was given a nice tour, introduced to nice staff and students, given another nice lunch and made more nice plans for my nice network. On my fourth day ...

Okay, let's stop there. The events depicted in the above couple of paragraphs didn't happen that way. They're a fictionalised account of how my trip *could have* played out had there been none of the shitty stuff that's happening to me in reality right now. It's a thought experiment and if it was as boring for you to read as it was for me to write, then I've made my point. If everything had been as easy as the tedious narrative above then I would have derived no meaning from it, from Manson's standpoint. Plus, how soon would I have begun to self-sabotage, supposing McGowan and Lacan are right about all of us secretly yearning for what spooks or stresses us? And what quality of articles, books or research projects would I have produced off the back of this cakewalk? Not a very high one, perhaps.

4

I have the same concern about self-sabotage now as I slope through the mall to my actual lunch date with actual Jejo and actual Manny. Whatever evasive action my conscious self will take to halt the anxiety, my unconscious self might thwart it, if it's so invested in the value of suffering. But I can't afford that mindset. McGowan might be right about satisfaction being unreachable over the long range, but I know that my anxiety comes in waves. I just want this current one to end by finding a safer space.

I spot an opportunity to do that: a poster in a shop window offering free blood pressure tests. The shop sells mobility aids for the elderly and disabled. The walking sticks and bags-with-wheels hanging from the ceiling remind me of a delicatessen's strung-up Italian sausages and chains of garlic. A guy in a light blue onesie and a soul patch fastens the cuff around my bicep. I breathe slowly, command myself to stop fidgeting.

'*Ang galing*,' the guy beams. '120/80.'

'At least I won't cark it from a heart attack any time soon,' I mumble. What I don't say is that there remain one thousand and one other worries about what I might die of.

5

At the bottom of any anxiety spiral is death – or terror thereof. I imagine my final moments and wish for them to be painless. 'I don't mind dying,' quipped Woody Allen. 'I just don't want to be there when it happens.' What will my final words be? Nothing banal, please. The Roman Emperor Vespasian, a renowned wit, reputedly said, 'Am I a god yet?' Groucho Marx checked out with, 'Die my dear? Well, that's the last thing I'll do.' If I can't come up with anything so amusing, what does it matter anyway? I'll soon be dust. And so will you. We all will.

I've watched two people close to me die from cancer – my uncle John and my friend Gareth. As soon as they were diagnosed, they were informed they had months left. Can there be a more anxiety-effecting experience? All plans, big and small, go out the window. At times they were overwhelmed by feelings of futility. At one point Gareth told me that, after a lifetime of seeking spiritual insight, he was disappointed at how banal waiting to die was. He and John both regretted having lived full lives, to employ the euphemism. Gareth said that a mutual friend, who was in the throes of substance addiction, shouldn't 'make the same mistakes that I made'. I'd never heard him question the bohemian lifestyle before.

As no stranger to excess myself, I've ruminated on how many blows the human body can take before it finally gives way. What damage accrues from each pint drunk, each cigarette smoked, each lungful of pollution inhaled, each blob of junk food scoffed? If only there were a test you could take to ascertain how close you are to that point of no return. Do you have weeks, months or years to turn your life around before the *really* bad stuff befalls you? Some get away with drinking and smoking themselves daft well into their eighties. So what else are they doing to offset the harm? People who achieve longevity often cite small portions of food as their secret. Genes play a part, too, within environmental bounds. You might be born with a strong heart, but you'll void that advantage with enough absinthe, speedballs and Cheese Footballs.

I've noticed that Indian writers and economists from all over the world seem to live longer. R.K. Narayan made it to 94, Balamani Amma 95, Malk Raj Anand 99. Still going strong are Amartya Sen, 91, and Thomas Sowell, 94, while Milton Friedman got to 94 and Ronald Coase reached a whopping 103. Do vegetarianism and prudence keep the Grim Reaper at bay? If so, I'm screwed. Others seem to go unjustly young such as all those great musicians aged 27. Then again, they were doing life-threatening things from the get-go. Reggae artists and rappers have met especially grim and premature ends. Tenor Saw was killed in a hit and run when he was a whippersnapping 21. Peter Tosh was murdered aged 42 by home invaders, Prince Far I by robbers when he was a few months shy of 40. I can think of no fewer than eight hip-hop stars, amongst them the twentysomething Tupac Shakur and Biggie Smalls, who were iced in gang violence.

If fear of death is inherent to life and at the root of anxiety, then maybe it gets supercharged when brought into contact with travel. I'm sure I'm not the only person who's imagined checking out miles from home, the indignity of a grieving relative crossing continents to fetch my corpse, supposing it hasn't rotted away somewhere. Travel presents us with perhaps six million ways to die – to quote the Jamaican dancehall singer Cutty Ranks, who is still going strong at 60 – especially if your itinerary includes war zones or extreme sports. Even the notion of going missing – as a lot of travellers do every year – is enough to give most people the willies.

There doesn't seem much we can do about death – which will come to everyone unless there's a breakthrough in immortality research – other than start to feel comfortable about it, as the Buddhists do. That takes work. Outside of their dark moments, John and Gareth had come to accept their upcoming quietus. Both spent the time they had left on self-improvement and righting wrongs. They wanted to go without regrets. They read as many books, listened to as much music and watched as many films as they could. They developed a new lust for life – or the aspects they were still able to savour – because they had so little time.

After his diagnosis, Gareth moved in with his daughter and son-in-law so that they could look after him. Despite his declining mobility, he had the best Christmas ever, in his words. It was his last and he made the most of it. Later, when he was bedridden and weary, we'd still have exhilarating conversations about literature, music, art, nature, politics and spirituality. In this sense, little had changed between us from all the years we'd spent down the pub. With his paint-spattered shirt and veteran rock star looks he always cut a cool, free-spirited figure. As a student of the human condition, he'd listen intently to anyone – whatever their creed or background – especially if they had an unusual story to tell. He'd be particularly intrigued if the story involved travelling somewhere he hadn't been. Although usually reserved Gareth could be blunt with those who indulged in egotism, pretension or one-upmanship. After witnessing some blokeish, beer-fuelled argument about a political issue or abstract concept, he'd say to me, 'Well, what's the emotion behind the rhetoric?' And if the emotion was petty or vindictive then he'd suggest that whoever was pushing it should do some self-examination before judging anybody or anything else. In that same vein, Gareth was mindful of his own feelings and motives – he strove to be himself and respected others who did likewise.

For someone who was now stuck in one place and unlikely to go anywhere else again, Gareth had a glittering trove of travel memories to draw on. He grew up in Hampshire and St Louis, Missouri, and later picked peaches on a kibbutz in Israel. One morning, after seeing Israeli tanks on the horizon as the Six-Day War was breaking out, he sensibly quit the job and hitchhiked back to the UK. The experience didn't put him off further wandering – later he'd visit Eastern Europe, North Africa, India, Iraq, the Bahamas and New Zealand, amongst other places. He held an academic post in Canada and taught English in the Libyan section of the Sahara Desert where he devoured the works of Dickens and Trollope, both of whom he'd love for the rest of his life. By the time I'd come to know him, he was also fond of travelogues by Robert Byron, Patrick Leigh Fermor and Laurens van der Post; mystical and religious texts from the

New Testament to Rumi's poetry; autobiographies (never one for 'high'/'low' cultural distinctions, he'd read everyone's from Tony Benn's to Nigel Benn's); and the post-colonial novels of Salman Rushdie, Rohinton Mistry and J.M. Coetzee. Gareth was probably the best-read person I've ever met.

In those last weeks of his life, I'd bring him the remaining couple of Trollope novels he hadn't read – he wanted to achieve this before checking out. He reached out to estranged friends, relatives and ex-partners and apologised for anything untoward he may have said or did in the past. I think I would want to end my own life with minimal regrets and loose ends. It would provide an appropriate ending to my story. And, on the off chance there is an afterlife, I wouldn't want to spend eternity in it full of regrets and recriminations.

When I saw him on the night before he passed, Gareth remarked on how beautiful the birdsong outside his room was. This took me back to the strolls we used to take around the Hampshire village of Rowlands Castle. The following morning, when I heard the news that he'd gone, I looked out of my window and thought that this was exactly the kind of bright, sunny spring day that would have stirred the pair of us to go up to Stansted Park and see the bluebells in blossom. He loved the bluebells.

6

I meet Jejo, a leading journalist, and Manny, a leading anthropologist, outside a glass cube canteen. Its sign, 'Tropical Hut TM', is in a kitsch, flowing, handwritten font and set against a lime-green neon background. If this is supposed to amuse or reassure patrons, it's not working on me. Nothing would, to be fair.

We take a Formica table and Jejo asks if I like Filipino fried chicken.

'Absolutely,' I proclaim. I go quiet as I think of an excuse not to eat much. The classic one is stomach upset – but then how will I warrant ordering beer? On a diet? My companions won't be persuaded by my chunky frame. Besides, there are more calories in the three bottles of San Miguel I'm about to chug than in a portion of crispy wings. 'I had a brunch meeting earlier,' I lie.

Jejo and Manny both smile faintly. I'm not sure what that means as their eyes – which are always so crucial to deciphering body language – remain neutral. If they'd widened or narrowed or rolled then that would probably mean 'you're full of shit'. Instead, I'll take it as 'we politely accept your explanation even if we doubt it'.

The food arrives. I'm worried about choking, about not properly working the muscles in my throat to send the food safely down. I chew every mouthful into baby-food consistency and chase it with beer. As I try to follow my colleagues' chat about the new Marcos presidency and the ongoing threat of Covid in the Philippines, my mind flashes back to when I have actually choked on a hunk of sourdough bread or a morsel of underdone steak or that fishbone that somehow got inserted like a splinter into the flesh of my epiglottis, and meant that I had to push my finger down to pull it out, causing me to retch blood. I can't dispel that frantic sensation at failing to breathe from the blockage and being minutes away from death if I couldn't dislodge it. What a lame byproduct of evolution, this minuscule space with which to do something so vital. Why didn't natural selection give us throats the width of wind tunnels?

Even when drinking my fragrant *sinigang* soup – a dish I'd adore in a better mood – I take care to ingest a tiny spoonful at a time, which draws suspicious looks from Jejo and Manny. Perhaps to ease the awkward vibe – or distract from it – Jejo asks, amid an exuberant munch of garlic rice, 'What do you think of your new king?'

I pause, holding my spoon an inch from my lips. I'll need to answer him first before returning my focus to eating. 'I'm a republican, don't care.' I squeeze out the phoniest of laughs to hopefully compensate for my reply being perceived as brusque. Should it be perceived that way. Which I hope it hasn't. Because it wasn't meant to be.

'Ever since we moved to England my wife has loved the royal family,' says Manny. 'But I think they're an anachronism.'

I swig more beer, craving emotional equilibrium. Are my companions thinking, *Is he an alcoholic? Can I trust this guy?*

'Did you want to start the interview now?' asks Jejo.

'Er, shall we …' I drop my spoon and reach for my pen and notebook. 'Maybe … er …'

'It's okay,' he says, 'we can socialise today and do the interview another time.'

'Sure, fine, excellent,' I jabber. 'We'll do that instead.'

After he takes his final bite, Jejo says, 'When I went to Popeye's in London, I was shocked at how much food was left. Whole chicken breasts, portions of French fries, bowls of beans thrown away.'

I glance furtively at my plate to three monumental king prawns, a palm-sized dollop of *ampalaya* salad and the khaki zigzag of a chicken wing. It's hard not to take Jejo's comment as a barely veiled putdown.

7

By the time Manny and I grab a cab back to Quezon City, the booze has settled me into what I call tolerable anxiety. I'm still jittery, but the doom-shadows have receded a bit. At least I can have a conversation now. Against my wishes, we stray onto the topic of academic work. Manny says he feels insecure next to his colleagues who are publishing more than him and getting bigger grants. His research record is impressive, so I wonder if he's as prone to undervaluing himself as I am. I'm glad to interrupt this joyless exchange with a visit to a branch of the National Bookstore. Shopping for Filipino literature in English lifts my spirits for the first time in thirty-six hours. I'm weird like that.

I go into what Mihaly Csikszentmihalyi coined as a 'flow state', an agreeable frame of mind the opposite of anxiety. Immersing yourself in an activity – especially a creative one like painting or playing an instrument – distracts you from the money, career and relationship worries of everyday life and the pressures of trying to please others. You lose track of time, like you did in childhood when playing in an imaginary world. You're focused purely on the present, not a prisoner of your regrets about the past or your fears for the future. The crucial thing about achieving flow is that it must be based on 'intrinsic motivation', i.e. doing the activity *is* the activity's reward – nothing more, nothing less, nothing else. Oscar Wilde summed it up most eloquently with his oft-misunderstood dictum, 'All art is quite useless.' By that he didn't mean that art was crap or that it was pointless to pursue, but rather that the virtue of creativity is that it doesn't have a clear, material end in the sense that other human activities like working or eating or procreating do. 'A work of art is useless as a flower is useless,' Wilde clarified. 'A flower blossoms for its own joy. We gain a moment of joy by looking at it.'

We gain joy from an activity only if it's not a means to an extrinsic end. If I'd spent half an hour combing through the National Bookstore's shelves with the aim of impressing Manny, or if I thought it would make me appear to be clever or right-on to the other customers, or if I thought I'd be able to buy some books and sell them on for a profit back in the UK, then I would not have accessed a flow state for a single damn second. Flow requires you to stow away your ego and all its associated baggage.

I lose myself in a book that reproduces the paintings of Fernando Amorsolo. His chiaroscuros of the Philippine countryside are at once concretely detailed and hazily impressionistic – a seductive interplay between realism and idealism. Born during the independence movement, Amorsolo helped create a nationalist mythos of placid yet dutiful peasants working flow-like in divine valleys, orchards and paddy fields. I find these natural images a respite from the very unnatural streets that I braved earlier. If anxiety can be spawned by an incredulity towards – and a feeling of powerlessness over – the fact that humans have made such a shambles of the cities they have built themselves, then places not created by humans compel us to be humbler and more pragmatic about life. As Alain de Botton observes, 'Sublime landscapes, through their grandeur and power, retain a symbolic role in bringing us to accept without bitterness or lamentation that which we cannot overcome and the events that we cannot make sense of.'

Although I'm not visiting the green and earthly locations that so dazzled Amorsolo, I find peace and beauty and wonder in his depictions of a firework-like sunrise mirrored on a moss-specked lagoon and a soaring ebony volcano which grows more enticingly opaque the higher it reaches into porcelain clouds. As if by touching each colour-plated page, I absorb some of this peace and beauty and wonder into my being. Or that's how it seems, anyway.

Only when Manny says he must head back to his hotel thereby ending our book-browsing and my flow state, do I realise that I've been in a flow state. A sure sign you've been in a flow state is that you're so immersed in it that you're not aware of it. You certainly don't try to quantify or explain it while you're in it. The problem is, now the flow state has gone, I'm back to feeling anxious. I was hoping – probably ambitiously – that even a half-hour dose of flow might vanquish the longer-range dread.

How the hell can I retrieve that flow state? Keep looking at the books? I've seen all the ones that interest me and, anyway, the shop will be shutting soon. I have the briefest – and quirkiest – fantasy of bribing the manager to let me stay on after they've locked the doors and turned out the lights …

'Are you coming?' asks Manny, perhaps for the third time.

8

My hotel occupies most of a condominium with a café in a ground floor unit. I think I can eat something now. Both fruit and savoury salad are on the menu but neither have been available since I checked in three days ago. I worry that vitamin lack is contributing to my head-fuckage. I order stir fried tofu and vegetables, which turns out to be cataclysmically short of vegetables and is mostly tofu and pork. You can't avoid pork in the Philippines, and it's usually tasty, though not what I want right now.

With Jejo's gripes about white people wasting food still ringing around my skull, I leave half the stir-fry and a fistful of rice. I take six overpriced bottles of San Mig Pale Pilsen up to my room where I decide to drink myself merrier. Over the years, I've found alcohol a fix for travel anxiety. In the short-term, at least. I'm a happy drunk – why bother if you're not? – who gains from it the courage to talk to strangers or venture somewhere risky at night. If anxiety is a colossal bypass of one's humour about everything then the old shant, as we call it in Portsmouth, puts me into an intensely frivolous headspace. My priorities flip upside down so that the things I fret about in the sober world – my loved ones, my job, social and ecological breakdown – stop mattering and instead I get engrossed in trivia, be it a round of pool in a pub, a colloquy on the relative merits of crisp flavours or a Google-dive into a widely forgotten ZX Spectrum computer game I was addicted to as a kid. When sozzled I come up with jokes and puns – poor ones, I grant you – and impressions that are even poorer. If sozzled enough, I'll inflict you with an even poorer karaoke performance.

Oscar Wilde said, 'Alcohol, taken in sufficient quantities, may produce all the effects of drunkenness.' To link this adage to his earlier one about art, the flow of beer can engender a flow state akin to childish diversion. One reason why drinking is so popular amongst adults is that it frees them from hang-ups rare in kids, like the terror of being judged by others. We crave those qualities that come easier to bairns. 'They're more alive, they're more perceptive, they're doing more, they're more vigorous and more vivid ...' as the children's author T.H. White framed it. Let's not whitewash this, though – people on the piss can also ape the shabbiest behaviours of kids, from petulance to bullying to stealing a traffic cone, vomiting in it and then wearing it on your head while you run away from the police. Come on, we've all done that, haven't we?

I thankfully reach that point – you know it – of cosy intoxication when the warmth seeps into your temples and a dumb smile creeps across your face and you can bear to watch Giles Coren for more than five minutes without wanting to fire a portable rocket launcher at the screen that his smug mug is currently darkening. Instead, I fall asleep to Mr Coren prattling on about posh hotels.

9

On this trip my sleep pattern has been mutilated by a Swiss Army knife of anxiety, drunkenness, humidity and jet lag. Wide awake at 5am, I try in vain to read, watch and doom-scroll myself back to sleep. It'd be better to prep for my upcoming visit to the university but I'm trying to be easier on myself when travelling. Previous sojourns to the Philippines have been gruelling work-wise, with interviews and archive digs booked from morning to night. Much of that time would be drained in traffic jams and I'd often be home around midnight. These were two-week trips in which I was working fifteen or sixteen hours a day. Burnout might have contributed to my hospitalisation in 2018. I don't want a repeat of that.

I rise at 6 and go for a walk. An old woman is crouched naked on the pavement over what look like pagan votives. Incense sticks are burning beside a packet of M&Ms and hunks of meat and fish. The woman picks a pebble up from the ground and puts it in her mouth. I'm worried that she'll end up poisoned and/or convicted of indecent exposure. A younger woman passes, pushing a boy in a wheelchair.

'Excuse me,' I say to them. I gesture to the old woman with my thumb. 'Is there anything we can do for her?'

The young woman shakes her head. 'Our government does not provide.' She carries on.

I walk on, looking around for help. Who can I alert? A police officer? A passing ambulance? A wandering emergency mental health worker? I chance upon the entrance of a private hospital. I ask the receptionist if they have a psychiatric unit.

'Sorry, sir, the care for people like that depends upon the mayor's attitude. Our mayor's attitude is not good.'

'Can't you just see her for a while? Give her some medication?'

'Does she have insurance?'

'I strongly doubt it.'

I try to look at things from the old woman's perspective. It's unusual to see a Filipino bereft of family support and cast onto the streets, whether they have health insurance or not. Her only hope might be that the gods notice the bits of food she's laid out for them. I consider asking if she needs anything. I'll probably just scare her.

Instead, I order breakfast at a pavement diner. The waitress has slashes of blonde in her black hair. 'Where from, sir?'

'UK.'

She's Ani and very talkative. She tells me that her boyfriend is English. He's 71, diabetic and recently had his legs 'cut' – by which I think she means amputated – so she's afraid he'll never return to Manila to see her. Eager to unburden herself, Ani says that she still loves him but was aggrieved when she discovered that he'd lied about his wife – also a Filipina – being dead. He was rumbled when the wife called the apartment he and Ani were sharing and Ani picked up the phone. The boyfriend then confessed to having a daughter that he'd never mentioned before.

'Could you travel to the UK to see him?' I ask.

She shrinks back. 'I cannot afford.'

I take a seat opposite a skinny bald Western guy bashing at the screen of a tablet with his thumbs. 'Goddamn thingamajig,' he says in a Euro-American accent. He looks up and catches my eye. 'Hey, I'm Eddie.'

'I'm Tom. Having trouble there?'

'You a techie? Goddamn touchscreen busted.'

'Afraid not.'

'Just visiting?'

'For a couple of weeks. You?'

'I moved here from Japan last year.'

'How does Manila compare?'

'Whole bunch better here. Food especially.' I expect him to extol the virtues of Filipino cuisine. 'Here you got Denny's, McDonald's, Kenny Rogers, Burger King. Can't go long without steaks and burgers and schnitzels.'

'Where are you from?'

'Parents are Swiss. Moved to the US when I was twelve.'

'You didn't get on with Japanese food?'

'Never tried it. Was 21 years there working in sales and never ate sushi or wagyu or anything like that.' He looks pleased with himself. 'Had a Japanese girlfriend for most of that time. Went to Kyoto with her.'

'A fascinating city, I hear.'

'Not to me. Whole goddamn place could have burned down, for all I care. Could have burned down with my girlfriend *in it*.' He laughs at that. I try not to look like I'm cringing.

Our respective orders arrive – fried *bangus* (milkfish) for me, fluffy American pancakes for him. As Eddie munches mechanically like Pacman, maple syrup running down his chin, my reflex response is ill will. How hidebound to spend over twenty years living somewhere and take no interest in the culture – or worse, openly despise it. He isn't the first expat to be guilty of this. I met plenty of others while backpacking around Southeast Asia in the noughties, which many bozos of my generation did. In Candi Dasa, a beach town in Bali, I stayed in a hostel run by an Australian called Coop and his local wife, Ida. He'd hold court in the outdoor restaurant each mealtime in a low, scratchy voice that made him sound like a conspirator from a Le Carré novel. He was usually topless, a bypass scar running between his breasts like a tie down to his bathtub belly. A cigarette was permanently pivoting in his mouth.

'The thing about Candi Dasa, right, is we've got the best beach in the world 'cept no one knows about it ... Mick Jagger and Jerry Hall got married just up the road ... My wife's a bloody wiz in the kitchen – it'll be just like your granny's cooking back in England ...'

He'd worked as a baggage handler for Qantas until a heart attack made him rethink everything. He flew to Bali and never came back. In Australia, he'd been a nobody. 'It was hard for a bloke to get on,' he moaned. 'Too many immigrants taking all the jobs.' With no concern for irony – or hypocrisy – Coop built a successful business here in Bali, putting his 'raconteur's skills' – his description – to use. He reminded me of Ronald Merrick, the colonial policeman in Paul Scott's Raj Quartet novels. Merrick felt his grammar school education and lack of connections impeded his career in Britain, so he moved to India where he could excel. Thousands of real-life expats would agree.

Like Merrick's superior attitude to Indians, Coop disliked the Balinese he lived amongst. He reserved special ire for those taxi drivers who dared to ask him for a 12,000 Rupiah (about 90p) tip. He didn't respect his wife much – she'd mostly be slaving away in the kitchen while he hung out half-naked, nattering, smoking and swigging Bintang beer.

One twilight, an ancient bloke whose knee joints creaked like under-lubricated brakes, joined us. 'This is Clive,' said Coop. 'He's a Kiwi, but please don't hold that against him.' Trailing behind Clive was a Balinese girl young enough to be his granddaughter. She was in fact his new wife. I didn't believe her claim to have children from a previous marriage. Clive had three grown-up sons of his own. They, too, had a penchant for Asian women.

'My eldest married a Japanese,' he said. 'My second a Vietnamese. But my youngest, well, he's been a disappointment to me – he married an Australian.' Coop tutted at the comeback. Clive winked.

The two men settled into the subject of intercultural relationships. Coop mentioned a retired Dutchman who'd moved into the area. 'He's bought the land, he's built the house, now he's looking for the girl. He'll find one no worries, bloke like that.'

After Clive and his missus retired, Coop disclosed a grimmer facet to expat relationships. 'That bloke you just met,' he said, leaning over his shoulder to ensure Clive was out of earshot, 'he had another Balinese sheila before that one. Got her pregnant. One night they were staying here and she wouldn't, you know, sleep with him. So he yelled at her, really upset her. Then he drove down to Kuta for a "takeaway". Know what he meant by that?'

I thought I did. 'What did you say to him?'

Coop stubbed out his cigarette. For the first time in three days, he was lost for words. 'Well ... well, what can you say? It's a hard one, but ... None of my business, mate.'

Below its blithe surface, Coop's industry was sinister – and he knew it. The imperatives of hospitality had made him a coward. He'd let someone behave like that so long as they were a paying customer. Would he have reacted differently to a Balinese man doing exactly the same thing to his girlfriend? Perhaps not – business can be colour blind.

The nineteenth-century wit Ambrose Bierce's wry definition of 'exile' could apply to an expat like Coop or Clive: 'One who serves his country by residing abroad, yet is not an ambassador.' Australia and New Zealand were well-served by these men residing over 1,000 miles from them.

Coop finished his eighth Bintang with a thunderous burp. I felt for poor Ida. His disdain for the locals – his hosts – applied to her, too, despite him calling her his 'true love'. He'd already had one heart attack and was due another if he carried on like this.

Coop must have had his fair share of anxieties. After his brush with mortality he must have been scared of the Angel of Death, yet he couldn't quit the lifestyle that would hasten that fate. I sympathised with him here, given my own battles. His contempt for the Balinese could hardly come from a sea of tranquility, nor his role as the innkeeper who did nothing so that evil could triumph. His anxiety made him act in ways that made others anxious: his long-suffering wife; the abused wives of his guests; locals who came away from his company patronised and insulted.

I contrast this lesson learned from Coop with a conversation I had with Lily in a peach-walled bar in Goa that used to be a Portuguese villa. Her peroxide blonde hair and sequined dress recalled a magician's assistant. Before us a band was tuning up. I asked her how she came to live in these parts.

She looked over at the band, tears rising in her heavily shadowed eyes. 'I'm sorry, it's been a while since somebody asked me that question.' She caught one of her tears – the size of a raindrop – in a napkin.

She told me she used to be a 'workaholic miser' who ran old people's homes in Auckland, New Zealand. When her twenty-year-old son Doug died in a car crash, she had a 'kind of breakdown' and stopped caring about her career and money.

She moved to Australia and lived on a houseboat. She threw lavish parties for her neighbours, enjoying this 'new feeling called generosity'. A typical bash would start with a steak and champagne breakfast and end with skinny dipping in the Timor Sea.

Lily then lived on a houseboat in Thailand for two years before sailing on a cargo ship to Goa. 'I was running away from something,' she said to me, but didn't mention her son. Her latest act of generosity was to buy instruments for the band before us, which had just started playing.

'Doug loved music,' she shouted in my ear. 'Really loved it.' For the first time this evening she smiled. Some other expats joined us, kissing Lily on the cheek. She kept smiling for the whole of the gig.

Lily's flight from the pain of her loss was healthier than Coop's, it seemed. Travel helped her to face off her demons, though she still wasn't rid of them by the time I met her and maybe never would be. Her response to her own blues was to give others a good time, give something to the world that could fill the gap left in it by her son's death.

10

Back in the present and watching Eddie chomping on his pancakes, the longer I think it over with my anxiety-infused brain, the more compassionate I feel towards him. Just as some have 'gaydar', a telepathic ability to ascertain if someone is LGBTQ+, I think I have 'feardar', insofar as I can tell a fellow anxiety-sufferer without having to ask. Perhaps Eddie was ordered by his company to Japan rather than it being his free choice and the comfort foods he grew up with allayed his homesickness. No harm in that, I suppose. On the other hand, wishing his girlfriend had died in a fire in Kyoto is a bit much.

I jump in a taxi driven by a man with a splendidly substantial mullet like a tractor's mudguard. He lifts up his mask to request that I put on mine. I've left it in the hotel. The driver gives me a spare one in a sealed packet.

At the university I'm greeted by the dean of the faculty and some senior academics. We go into a boardroom, its air con buzzing like outraged insects. On a long table is a plate of Dunkin' Doughnuts and paper cups of coffee.

'Please, enjoy some breakfast,' says the dean.

This opens me up to some potential faux pas. I'm allergic to coffee, so respectfully turn that down. It's okay, they have tea as well. A male academic with a permanent beatific grin says, 'I have worked in the UK and I know how you Brits like your tea.' I'm not hungry after my early breakfast and wouldn't normally scoff a doughnut for health reasons. Filipinos often assume that if you're a Westerner then you must like the Western fast-food chains that have been exported here. I don't want to offend so I pick the least decadent-looking of the dainties.

Though it's hard to hear her above the racket of the air-con, the dean gives me a potted history of the institution. She then asks me why I got interested in the Philippines. The grinning academic films me on his phone as I answer. This introduces some stage fright. 'My grandfather served in Asia in the Second World War,' I say. 'He used to tell me stories of docking at Manila and that made me interested in this part of the world. I realised later that Grandad had a rather reactionary and colonial attitude to the Philippines, so my own perspective was nuanced by reading Filipino novelists and academics.' Nods and smiles all round. I've passed some test, it seems.

The dean casts open palms around the room. 'Do you think this will be an appropriate venue for the workshops, Dr Tom?'

To cement the relationship between our institutions I've proposed a series of workshops bringing together journalists and media academics in the UK and the Philippines. 'Do you have wifi here?' I ask.

'Yes, but it is intermittent.'

'That can be the case at my university, too. How about a big screen that we can use to show slides?'

'Not in this room, I am afraid.'

I try my damnedest not to imagine a situation where academics are struggling to hear each other speak and going off at the deep end because they can't log onto their Powerpoint presentations, let alone show them. 'I'm sure we'll be fine.'

I'm taken on a tour of some excellent facilities. There are TV and radio studios, a dark room for photography and plenty of IT workstations. We pause for something of a photo-shoot, with a student running around with a camera asking us to pose like this, pose like that. At the end, the dean inspects the pictures. 'I think I look better in 2-D,' she giggles.

Since she's a former reporter I ask her what the major news stories are in Manila just now. She suspects that the new president, Bongbong Marcos, is covering up the true extent of Covid infections. 'Misinformation is at his core,' she adds, alluding I think both to his election campaign, which mobilised trolling and fake news on an epic scale, and his parents' yen for misleading the public about their myriad crimes.

'People are very disciplined about wearing masks and keeping their distance,' I say.

'Yes, some good information is filtering through.'

11

At midday, five of us get into an SUV and drive along the arterial EDSA road. The dean shows me a video on her phone that she uses to teach PR. It's about a couple of young guys who pulled a very digital-era hoax by designing a website for a trendy London restaurant that didn't exist. Through canny use of social media, involving fake reviews and the like, they convinced hipsters and food critics that they were the next big thing. The guys became so famous that they were compelled to put on a gala night. They laid out some ramshackle tables and chairs on the roof of the house they rented, claiming that this was some new guerrilla dining concept, and served their VIP guests baked beans and instant noodles. They got rave reviews, such was the hype around the bistro-that-never-was. The theme of this escapade – pretending to be something that you're not – is a bit too close to home as I'm feeling the burden of representing my university on this high-stakes visit. I can't be myself – I'm not Tom as much as I'm At-Work Tom, Ambassador Tom. But the dean's laughter is infectious and I'm soon able to see the funny side of the documentary.

We're joined by another dozen colleagues in the restaurant of a country club. On the Sykes Scale – a scale for measuring travel anxiety that I've just invented – I'm probably a two out of ten at this point. This is not unusual given the task at hand. There's a small but necessary degree of nerves around how smart I look, about the credibility of the answers I give to questions and all that jazz. I'm reminded of what the veteran broadcaster David Dimbleby said when asked if he still got nervous after twenty years presenting *BBC Question Time*. He most certainly did, he snapped, and would be worried if he didn't, lest complacency creep in and he'd not do his job properly.

That being so, as per the internal reward system many of us operate by, I believe I've worked hard this morning and I deserve to turn the dial down to one or why not zero. I order a San Miguel Light and hope my hosts – all of whom plump for soft drinks – don't hate me for it. That first bottle goes down too easily as the waiters bring exquisite platters of *sisig* (a sizzling hodgepodge of meat, chilis and fried egg), *lechon* (suckling pig), crispy *pata* (deep-fried pig trotters) and *kare-kare* (the signature dish of a Filipino-Indian community derived from sepoys who deserted the British army when it occupied Manila in 1762–64). I enter a flow state, of sorts, that comes from being in good company, eating good food and drinking good beer.

After we eat, we flop on sofas in a reception room with a delightful view of Manila's skyline. All of a sudden, I don't feel so well. *Not fucking again,* I rage to myself. *Didn't I leave this bollocks at the mall yesterday?* I daren't own up to being anxious – not yet at least – so I whisper to the dean, 'I'm terribly sorry but I'm feeling sick.' The country club is posh enough to have its own in-house nurse, a girl who doesn't look old enough to have studied for a medical qualification. She takes my blood pressure: 166 over 101. She asks me if I'm on meds. I tell her yes.

'Do you have your tablets with you, Dr Tom?' asks the dean.

'No.'

'You should. I always take mine wherever I go.'

The nurse says that she can't prescribe anything to me and that I should go to hospital.

'It'll pass,' I mumble.

'Why do you say that?' asks the dean.

'I'm prone to anxiety.'

The dean looks crestfallen. 'Why are you feeling anxious with us, Dr Tom? What have we done to make this happen?'

She's right in a way. Rationally speaking there's been nothing for me to worry about on this pleasant enough day of meeting and greeting pleasant enough people. A couple of months hence, though, in a therapy session my counsellor will correctly inform me that flying to the other side of the world to represent your institution in a major collaborative project might bring with it certain pressures, whether consciously acknowledged or not.

'It's ... it's nothing personal,' I say to the dean. 'My anxiety can come on when not expected. Can I have a glass of water, please?' I close my eyes and will it to pass.

'Yay, I am in the lead!' cries one of her colleagues, removing the cuff of the BP monitor from his arm. My hosts are playing a game of 'who has the healthiest blood pressure readings'. This makes me feel even more rotten.

After a minute the nurse takes my readings again: 162 over 99. Again, she advises hospitalisation. The dean nods and gathers up her coat and bag.

'Can I use the comfort room first?' I ask. The winner of the readings competition accompanies me, on the nurse's advice.

When I return, my BP is still mountain-high. The nurse calls for a stretcher.

'R-really, this isn't necessary.'

'Sir, we must take precautions.'

The effect embarrassment has on anxiety is equivalent to that of flinging meths on a barbecue. I cover my face as I'm wheeled out of the country club and into the back of the SUV. The academic with the beatific grin tries to keep my pecker up with jokes about 'another five pints sorting me out, as that is what you Brits are like'. I wish he'd just shut up.

After a quarter of an hour's drive, we pull into the car park of a clinic. The dean goes into the clinic and returns all too quickly. 'They are full up, no beds available.' She speaks in Filipino to the others. 'We will try somewhere else.'

At that moment, I snap out of it. Just like that. I'm back to a tipsy and talkative mode of being. We don't have a BP machine handy but I'm morally certain I'm back to a safe reading. 'Can you drop me at my hotel, please?'

'Are you sure, Dr Tom?'

'Positive.'

'Well, do not hesitate to call me if you have more problems.'

'Of course,' I say, but it's the last thing I'll do after today's shame-fest.

12

In the hotel lobby I scroll through the emails that have amassed in my inbox despite my 'out of office' message stating that I'm abroad on university business. I dwell on what the dean said earlier. '*Why are you feeling anxious with us, Dr Tom? What have we done to make this happen?*' I don't blame her, but her remarks point to the general ignorance about what anxiety is and how it works. The last thing the anxious traveller wants to hear is that their carry-on has upset or offended someone. That only pumps up the anxiety.

Accepting that this trip will involve peaks and troughs in my mood, I notice I'm going trough-ward again. I slam my laptop shut and order a Cerveza Negra, despite having vowed to myself that I wouldn't drink again today after my mini-crisis earlier. The mildly addicted mind will always find excuses to feed the mild addiction. I just want to get into a more placid headspace. I have another bottle. And then another. I'm no closer to that tipsy peak that I reached at lunchtime. If anything, I've slid further downhill from it.

I head up to my room and put on a film that I'd normally find engaging – *Goyo: The Boy General*, about the Filipino revolutionary Gregorio del Pilar. I can't concentrate. The symptoms are intensifying: the compulsive fidgeting, the hammering heart, the Velcro-like throat, the edgy ideations.

I stand up, pace my room. Should I buy a bottle of whisky at the bar, get the job done properly? Swigging myself to sleep could be a solution, though not a perfect one. I'd gladly trade several hours of mortifying nightmares for this present daymare. But sleep is the first casualty of anxiety. In this pickle, I could devour a distillery's worth of single malt and suck on Oliver Reed's liver for six hours … and still not be blotto enough to fall into the arms of the Sandman.

At the same time, I can't rely on self-medication. It'll only store up problems for tomorrow. My mind's eye spies an animated reconstruction – like those in the medical drama *House* – of my brain under attack from 'hangxiety'. Since I know little about science, my imagination runs amok. I see the giant walnut of my cerebrum turning yellow, desertifying from dehydration, while under siege from black and grey spheres of cortisol. The fluorescent dots of my serotonin and dopamine – my 'happy chemicals' – flee the battle. My glutamate's gone AWOL, too, shattering the morale of my neutrons and making them stand down from firing the electrical signals essential to brain health.

In the front pocket of my backpack is a carton of Propranolol that my GP prescribed me before I left the UK. It's a beta-blocker that slows down the heart and tackles anxiety symptoms such as shaking and sweating. At the time I asked my GP if I could give it a test run while not feeling anxious, to see if I got on with it. She said no, not a good idea, only neck it when feeling rough. Now I'm feeling *very* rough, but I don't want to try this drug for the first time in this situation. What if something bad happens? Google reports that you shouldn't mix Propranolol with alcohol – even though they almost rhyme. If there was someone to watch over me in case I fucked up, then I'd take it. But there isn't, so I'm anxious. I'm anxious about taking anti-anxiety medication. This is nuts. *I am* nuts. I could go downstairs and sit with the night clerk of the hotel, tell him to keep an eye on me and call an ambulance if needed. No, I couldn't, that would be just as nuts – not to say unfair on the poor guy. He's paid to sit at a desk all night, not babysit guests with mental health issues.

It's getting worse. I'm now sailing close to the treacherous Reef of Panic in a force ten storm in the good ship *What the*

Fuck is Happening to Me? While the 'think happy thoughts' approach hasn't often worked for me, I try it anyway, alongside all the other methods I've been taught. Control breathing. Focus on a detail in the room. Coping statements: *I'm fine. I'm not going to die. This, too, shall pass.*

I clamp my eyes shut. I try to blank the mind, cut off the thought stream. I can't do it. I picture myself in a post-apocalyptic world – and how useless I'd be. Then I see a dead-eyed drug dealer from my student days who overcharged my friends and me and fancied a girl I was seeing at the time. A horrible boss in a horrible telesales job I did in the academic holidays. Current misgivings about a new online marking system we've had to adopt at work. There's no connective tissue between the thoughts other than that they're all ghastly.

Some clinicians advise shouting 'stop' at negative thoughts. First, I mutter it, then I say it, then I shout it. I shout it again. If I'm overheard, the men in white coats might be alerted.

13

A few days ago I was feeling much better. This, despite the chaos I had to tolerate at three airports. The near-petrified queues at Heathrow that almost made me miss my flight were, an attendant told me, down to post-Brexit staff shortages and a huge demand for holidays after two years of Covid lockdowns. Employees of the King Khalid (Saudi Arabia) and Ninoy Aquino (Manila) airports also blamed the pandemic, though for problems surely not caused by it. Entering

King Khalid, I wearily queried why our bags had to be sent through three X-ray machines. 'New security regulations due to Covid, sir,' said the bearded, bandana'd aide. I'd have got in shtuck if I'd voiced my next question: *What's Covid got to do with terrorism?*

You haven't been able to say things like this at airports since 9/11. Osama bin Laden got what he wanted: the conversion of decadent Western air travel into a nightmare. He might have been a fan of the draconian regimes airports have become. Passengers are searched, interrogated, have harmless objects like bottles of water confiscated, and are herded around like the subjects of a police state – whether the airport's in a police state or not. Diktats bully you from screens, *Nineteen Eighty-Four*-style: 'Don't drink too much alcohol before your flight.' Another common command is: 'Don't ever make jokes about bombs.' Does it ever strike the aviation autocrats that a joke about a bomb might actually ease fears of flying? We are less scared once we name that which scares us – and laugh about it. Besides, only the world's most inept terrorist would openly joke about the bomb they're about to plant. It's the ones who stay markedly quiet about planting bombs we should fret over.

While I've experienced all the above, I've typically stayed calm in airports, anxious traveller that I am. I have other reactions that are almost as unwelcome. Sadness coupled with ire gripped me as I queued at immigration in Ninoy Aquino Airport. An overhead sign said that it was a crime to subject staff to 'physical or verbal assault'. The rule wasn't cutting both ways when I saw how a young woman in a hijab was being treated.

'How do you call yourself Filipino?' scoffed an immigration officer from behind his desk. He wore a barely plausible toupée the texture of the fluff that blocks up a vacuum cleaner.

The woman blinked and bowed her head.

'You don't even speak Tagalog,' said the officer, tapping her passport on the desk like a carton of cigarettes.

'Yes, sir,' the woman muttered.

The officer raised his voice. 'Excuse me? I can't hear you.' He glanced over to a colleague at the next desk along. She had a conspiratorial smile waiting for him. The male officer tapped the passport some more. He was enjoying his power. The woman wouldn't gainsay him or she'd be denied entry to the country, her *own* country. And no one else was going to challenge him on her behalf lest they be denied, too.

'You were born in Sabah, Malaysia and you call yourself a Filipino?' the officer sneers.

'Yes, sir.'

'What is the purpose of your visit?'

'I already told you, sir.'

'Tell me again.'

'To see my family, sir.'

The officer tapped her passport some more. He called off his power trip only when, from behind the woman, a more confident and middle-class Filipino couple told him they had a taxi to catch.

These feelings I had on my way to Manila were unpleasant but manageable. But perhaps they have snowballed into this enfeebled state I'm in now.

14

I dart down to the hotel reception. The clerk is asleep, baseball cap buried in crossed forearms. I have a compulsion to moisten my lips with my tongue before I say anything. 'I-I need a-a doctor.'

The man springs awake and blinks his left eye a few times, something stuck in it. 'Should I call ambulance, sir?'

'P-please.'

He rubs the afflicted eye and dials 911. He talks in Filipino for a bit. He puts the phone down. 'I advise taxicab, sir.'

I summon one on Grab, an Uber-like app popular in Asia. A private hospital is five minutes away on the midnight, almost traffic-free roads of Quezon City.

I lumber towards the entrance to A&E. A masked medic invites me to lie down on a rolling stretcher. I don't want to lie down. I'll feel too constricted. I sit on the stretcher instead.

'Please lie, sir,' says the doctor again. 'For your own safety.'

I do it. The walls of my throat are painfully frictive. 'C-can I have w-water?'

'Not yet, sir. Please wait.' Others mass around my trolley. I'm pushed inside the waiting room.

I'm given a mask. 'For Covid prevention, sir. What is the matter?'

The mask is on too tight, muffling my already quiet voice – I don't have the energy to make it louder. 'I'm d-dizzy, n-nauseous ...'

A masked medic opens my mask and shoves a straw between my lips. I'm wheeled into a ward where the traffic is as slow-moving as the daytime streets of Manila. On a tight corner, we play a gentle game of chicken with another stretcher carrying someone surely close to death – an almost translucently grey human shape with faint, fossil-like markings where features like eyes and ears should be. My bearers decide it's more urgent for the other stretcher to pass and back me up.

We stop amidst other machines on wheels. Wires are stickered to my chest, arms and legs. 'Can you stop shaking, sir?' I think they mean fidgeting. I focus with all my might to cut it out. I wince as a needle is stuck in my arm and a canula fitted.

Although I'm fairly sure I'm ill from anxiety, a part of me is hoping there's something physical wrong with me. I don't want history to repeat itself. I'm in the same hospital I was in four years ago and I don't want to be here with the same complaint. A physical trigger will be less humiliating than my carers discovering that my suffering is all in my head and could have been prevented with some therapy or meditation. I won't feel guilty about bed-blocking. Then again, isn't it society's problem if it doesn't regard mental distress as a 'real' disorder in the same way that it does a broken arm or a cardiac arrest?

A woman doctor appears with a clipboard. Condensation builds on her glasses as she talks through her mask. She asks me questions that she's probably asked a dozen times a day for decades. 'What is your name and date of birth?'

I tell her, but I'm not loud enough through the mask. It's getting harder to say anything in this state. *Are my lungs failing?* She asks me to repeat myself and I oblige.

'Are you currently taking any medications, Dr Tom?'

'Ramipril for b-blood pressure.'

Her eyes flip over to one of the machines. 'Your blood is rather high just now.'

'Sh-shit, is it?'

'Don't worry, we will give you something for it. Are you allergic to any medications?'

'N-no.'

'Pardon me?'

'No!'

'Have you been drinking alcohol?'

'A l-little.'

'How much?'

'A f-few beers. I-I'm not g-going to d-die, am I?'

The doctor studies me like I'm a rare specimen of complete stupidity. 'No, you're not going to die, Dr Tom. Are you a medical doctor yourself?'

'F-fat chance.'

'We will give you some Vitamin B to begin with.'

There's nothing like lying in a hospital to make you ponder whether anxiety is triggered by physical illness or whether physical symptoms are the result of anxiety. The cognitive psychologist Ulric Neisser found that panic attacks are often caused by a paranoid mistaking of trivial sensations – an ache here, a twinge there – for signs of a lethal malaise like a stroke. On the other hand, Peter Lang's 'three-systems' theory has shown that anxiety can trigger physical discomfort such as a racing heartbeat which can in turn bring chest aches and wooziness. (The other two manifestations of anxiety, for Lang, are in what we say and think, and in how we act.)

The doctor hands me some pills. I don't ask her what they are. I'm in a place of care and I'll take any care on offer. Just please make me better.

15

I'm at the wheel of an SUV. I've no clue what the buttons on the dashboard do. I can't reach the pedals with my feet. Somehow, I drive under an archway reading 'Barangay 249 – Mabuhay!' and into a fumy slum with refuse sacks heaped on one another like steppes. Above looms a whopping golf-ball-style edifice that smacks of capital and connectivity. The contrast between the two sights seems to say something about the inequities of a megacity like Manila.

A preschooler giving a toddler a piggyback ambles in front of me. Without my doing, the SUV swerves and the engine fizzles out. I'm dimly aware that the ignition must be turned to make these contraptions work, but I can't find it. Horns toot and people cuss at me.

The events in the two preceding paragraphs didn't happen. They constitute a recurring anxiety dream. The setting differs – could be a damp country lane in Hampshire or a snowy trunk road in Eastern Europe – but a fixture is the sudden realisation that I'm in control of a car that I don't know how to drive. By the way, I don't know how to drive in real life either. Yes, I'm a travel writer who can't drive and has a crap sense of direction. In real life, too, I've come to detest car travel, necessary evil that it is. Being in a car seat is so restrictive – at least on a train or a plane you can walk around. Stopping for the toilet in a car can be a horror show, as you need to wait for motorway services or a discreet side-road. Though the latrines aren't always pretty, at least you can use one when you need it on a train or plane.

According to surveys, up to 40 per cent of Britons have aerophobia (fear of flying) whereas amaxophobia (fear of driving or riding in a vehicle) affects only 6 per cent. However, you're 750 times more likely to die in a car crash than in a plane wreck. That makes me feel slightly vindicated. Psychologist Nicole Murphy has found that amaxophobia intersects with other common phobias including claustrophobia (acute fear of small spaces), agoraphobia (crowded places from which escape is tricky), tachophobia (speed), dystychiphobia (accidents), algophobia (physical pain) and thanatophobia (death). I'm subject to all those, too, but there's nothing so wrong with fearing pain and death, I reckon.

I wake from the vehicular feverdream in the hospital. The woman doctor appears and starts unplugging wires and tubes from me. 'We let you rest, Dr Tom.'

'Very kind of you.'

'Feeling better now?'

'Infinitely.'

She takes me to an office where I hand over my insurance details to a black-lipsticked cybergoth girl with what look like pink bicycle inner tubes woven into her hair.

In the taxi I agonise over whether to stay in Manila or go. While I feel better than ever, the last 48 hours have been concerning. I've had two panic attacks and a shit-ton of ongoing anxiety over that period. This is more than I've suffered in eighteen months.

On the 'stay' side of the equation I still have exciting appointments in Manila, including more journalistic interviews and a reunion with buddies I made ten years ago when I was living here. On the 'go' side I couldn't risk another social blunder on the scale of the academics' lunch, much less another hospital stay.

I contact my friend, a UK-based Filipina nurse, and start recounting the events of the last two days. I don't get far before she types, 'Come home, Tom.' That seals it.

PART 2. APPRENTICESHIP OF AN ANXIOUS TRAVELLER

1

It's ironic that someone who started travelling to overcome anxiety should become an anxious traveller. My earliest memory of travel anxiety didn't take place somewhere exotic or far-flung – I got lost in a Hampshire supermarket aged six. Even on tip-toes, I couldn't spot my mum's lower half amongst the waltz of shell suit bottoms, stonewashed jeans and cream chinos that adults wore in the mid-eighties.

I dashed around the shop, staring down the aisles of goods, many now obsolete – spray cans with aerosol gases in them, paint pots containing leads, sweets riddled with artificial 'E' colours, Betamax video tapes, Mastertronic computer games on cassettes. I came to a stop, my energy drained more by a sense of futility – I still couldn't find my mum – than physical tiredness. This was the first time I experienced what would become a hallmark of later anxiety, a sensation of the world compressing around me, being too much to bear and contemplate, depriving me of options, of freedoms. This morphed into a feeling of physical breakdown, of my heart struggling to beat, my lungs fighting to inhale and exhale. I catastrophised for perhaps the first time in my life. If I couldn't find my mum in the next few hours, where would I go? Would I have to sleep next to the fridge of Mattessons smoked pork sausages? Who would tuck me in and read me a bedtime story? Surely that was too much to ask of a supermarket shelf-stacker in 1985. Who would make me my dinner? If I was going to be stuck next to the sausages, could I graze on them? Then, further down the line, would I be carted off to some dilapidated Gothic children's home and fostered by abusive parents? I was a precocious kid who'd seen gritty documentaries about these places. Something else I learned that day was that if ignorance is bliss then a little too much knowledge is misery.

Out of misplaced shame or pride, I didn't want to present myself to a staff member and admit that I couldn't find my mum. In the end I did something way more embarrassing – I squatted down beside the cigarette kiosk and started sobbing. The sobbing did me good, like a release valve for all the pent-up panic.

I was saved by the supermarket's PA system. 'Would young Tom Sykes, that's Tom Sykes, please report to till number seven? Till number seven.' When I reached said till, my mum was surprisingly unflustered. What had felt to me like hours missing had in truth been a few minutes. I felt safe and complete again.

After that escapade, I made a resolution to be more confident about going places on my own. A few years later at a church jumble sale, I helped a frail old geezer pack books he'd bought into a polythene bag – also a rare item these days. He was tiny and had a drastic stoop so that, when he looked up to talk to me, his body bent in two directions like an S-hook. 'Give us a hand with this gear back to my place, would you, son?'

I was no boy scout, though out of simple civility I agreed. I seldom ventured anywhere outside of the company of friends and family, so walking up the road with this geezer was a minor adventure. When we came to his front door, I put his books down and he dropped a pound coin into my hand.

When I returned to the jumble sale my mum was hysterical. 'What the hell were you thinking?'

'I was only helping–'

'He's a convicted paedophile, for God's sake!'

'Nothing bad happened. I didn't go inside–'

'You shouldn't have gone with him at all!'

I couldn't believe the allegation. By the look of the old geezer he'd have struggled to molest a tortoiseshell butterfly – or any other insect that was quintessentially British then but is close to extinction now. 'How was I supposed to know?' I protested.

Mum threw her arms around my shoulders.

This early quest to reduce my anxiety through being more independent and going places I hadn't been had only sparked anxiety in someone else. I still feel guilty about it, but I think my mum has recovered.

Another sign of different times is the fact that a known nonce would be able to live in a British suburb without attracting a vengeful mob. Mum's tearful reaction might have put me off ever going anywhere again without supervision. But a couple of years later, I started walking from school at kicking-out time over to my grandmother's house fifteen minutes away. This was quite a coup for a timid adolescent. These sojourns would sometimes be hurried along by the pursuit of school bullies, though it was a price worth paying for more independence – and a much lower one than the insidious strain of anxiety that possessed me on Sunday evenings in the early nineties.

I'll always associate that with the glum, languorous midi theme tune of *Alex Kidd*, a Sega Master System videogame my younger brother and I played religiously. On Sundays I'd be worrying about what school tomorrow would bring, its bullies and boredom and brainwashing of us into Little England values. I was worried about being poorer than my peers and about my brother who, when asked by his teacher in front of the whole class what his favourite meal was, said 'beans on toast' and about a wealthier relative asking if the clapped-out hoover my mum used was an antique and her replying that it was the best we could afford. I was worried about having friends to visit because our house was rundown and full of hand-me-down appliances and had broken windows held together with masking tape like we'd copped a bomb in the Blitz. I was worried about my parents' recent divorce and blamed myself for it, as kids in that situation will. I was worried about having to divide my loyalties between Mum and Dad and had begun to idealise the latter since he wasn't around so much. Longer-term I was worried about exams and qualifications and getting a job – this being patterned by my own childhood experiences of having parents who, along with about 4 million other Britons, had been unemployed for large chunks of the eighties.

2

I dreamt of escape. This grew as I got older and less tolerant of the limited horizons of parochial Hayling Island. I yearned to travel. It would make me freer and more self-reliant and less vulnerable to the forces that had hobbled my parents. I've also come to associate travel with 'deluxe' activities we almost never did growing up such as staying in hotels and eating out. On the cheap holidays we took in my youth we camped or stayed at a friend's. I can count the number of slap-up curries and pub lunches I ate between the ages of zero and sixteen on the fingers of one hand.

My itch to travel took me not very far to university, first in London then in Norwich. That seemed to do the trick, as I don't recall much anxiety in those days. If anything, I thrived on the adrenaline gained from sitting exams – a classic fear-trigger for many – and dared myself to overcome shyness and make friends. While at uni, I met peers who'd taken a gap year to backpack around Asia, volunteer in Africa, work in a bar in Australia, help conserve llamas in Peru or, in one eccentric instance, go sightseeing in the countries that belonged to the 'Axis of Evil': Iraq; Iran; Libya; Syria; Cuba and North Korea. (I later found out that someone was jerking my chain about this and had plagiarised the story from a journalist who did this tour.) I might have envied these experiences, but I was too lazy to emulate them.

My idleness extended to being a ropey student – ironic for someone who became an academic later in life. In short, I partied too much and studied too little. Despite that, I clung on to the notion that the life of the mind was for me and thus I read a lot. One book that grabbed me was *The Sane Society* by the German philosopher Erich Fromm, first published in 1955 when Western working people were enjoying unheard-of prosperity and were in many ways better off than they are now. However, Fromm was nervous about his adopted America's obsession with economic production, which sent many into the hostile terrain of anxiety. Fromm tried to re-define mental health so that anyone who adapted to the then-new normal of inane and unstimulating work was probably sick. Conforming to 'an alienated world' meant giving up your agency, autonomy and capacity to '[live life] intensely, to be fully born, to be fully awake'. For Fromm, the capitalist machine could only give its cogs fleeting relief. The 'world of fun and amusement' available to the fifties Westerner was no cure for anguish-ridden workplaces: '... covering up a symptom does not do away with the conditions which produce it.'

When I graduated with no idea what to do but keep partying, Fromm's theories made sense of my first foray into work after uni. I was an entry level civil servant tasked with inputting names and addresses into a database. That was it. Work doesn't get much more meaningless and unstimulating than that, which is why it's probably now being performed by AI. I'd finish each day's workload by lunchtime and spend the afternoon playing computer games and reading online articles. Any hankering I had for a more fulfilling life – writing, travelling, making friends, meeting the right partner – withered away. I spent the evenings and weekends trying to forget about my bullshit job with drink and drugs. As Jonathan Haidt writes in his book *The Anxious*

Generation, 'There is a hole, an emptiness in us all, that we strive to fill. If it doesn't get filled with something noble and elevated, modern society will quickly pump it full of garbage.'

3

Sometimes this desperate pleasure-seeking seeped into my working day in a harmful fashion. Because I was good at pressing buttons on a keyboard – as the proverbial schooled simian would be – I was made to train new recruits in pressing buttons on a keyboard. Doing something astonishingly dull all day is bad enough, but teaching someone how to do something astonishingly dull all day will break the sanity of the most resilient. With one trainee – and I apologise to him now if he's reading this – I grew so bored that I went into a delirious mood as if I were on psychotropic drugs. I did silly voices, sang silly songs with silly lyrics made up on the spot and gave silly answers to the poor trainee's serious questions. I wondered if my absurdist fugue was some evolutionary safeguard kicking in to prevent a boredom-driven breakdown, not unlike a starving body starts devouring its fat reserves. 'Boredom is a disease worse than cancer,' says the stand-up comic Doug Stanhope. Hyperbole, to be sure, but with a grain of truth. Looking back, the nervous energy propelling my tomfoolery – my *Tomfoolery* – paralleled what would later underpin my anxiety. The physical symptoms were the same – the restlessness, the hurry, the accelerated thought processes – but they were free of foreboding. Be that as it may, I could tell that this wasn't a safe condition to be in. I finally shut up when my trainee informed me that he had an A-Level in psychology and thought I was bordering on the schizophrenic.

As each day went by in that McJob, details accrued in a mental picture of my future. I saw myself gaining promotion into more or less the same role I was doing already, only with different data to input – and the occasional opportunity to give a presentation about it. The prospect of being stuck in this sector for the rest of my working life, wasting eight hours of my time five days a week, was a bleak one. The bleakness wasn't allayed by the legion of older colleagues who described themselves as 'lifers', just like murder convicts. They'd stop at my desk and say things like, 'I wonder where the last 40 years have gone, I really do.'

After a year of inauthentic civil servitude, I was lying in bed on a Saturday afternoon recovering from a drum 'n' bass all-nighter when I found I couldn't breathe. I sat up and willed myself to inhale, the oxygen feeling like it was trying to force itself through my windpipe and lungs before concrete set in them. My vision was blurred and fractured, as if I were looking through steamed-up spectacles at a frosted beer glass. The sounds of a Justin Timberlake track coming from the flat above and a DIYer using a buzzsaw across the road congealed into one squelching, slurring drone like a cassette player almost drained of battery. I leaped to my feet and almost fell down again from dizziness. I gripped hold of the mantelpiece and focused on breathing. At the same time, I had the intense impulse to swallow, a warped inner voice telling me that if I didn't do this I'd die. But I couldn't summon any saliva and my throat was drier than a data-inputter's employment contract. I downed the rest of a bottle of Lucozade, not caring that spliff roaches had been marinating in it since four o'clock that morning.

I started to cool down and not because of the spliff roaches à la Lucozade. My breathing got easier. My vision de-iced. I could hear DIY and Justin Timberlake again but still struggled to tell the difference between them. Over the next few weeks, I tried to forget that this incident had ever happened. This was mostly because I wasn't sure what had happened. The incident had occurred chronologically far enough away from (and its symptoms were different enough) to that childhood freakout in the supermarket, that I didn't at the time see it as part of a longer narrative about how I became an anxious traveller – or anxious person generally. Nor would I be able to figure out until after the fact that these symptoms would be typical of future panic attacks. At the time I put that dismal episode down to a post-partying chemical imbalance in my head and so carried on partying and putting what I thought were the *right* chemicals in my head.

4

Six months later, I had a longer and more sustained bout of anxiety. Nowadays I'd term it mid-table anxiety. The symptoms were a lower-grade version of those I'd suffered on that Saturday afternoon plus some new ones. I was hyper-aware of my breathing and swallowing. There was a degree of dizziness and lethargy but not enough to immobilise me. A compulsion to keep moving around and, when I did sit down, shake my legs was, I now realise, the beginnings of agitation. I could function, just about – or as well as anyone can function without being able to sleep or concentrate on anything for very long. I was unemployed by this period, so at least I didn't have to try and act un-anxious in some workplace amongst judgy colleagues or complete a workload that I wouldn't have been able to focus on. Also new to the mix were symptoms that would become tiresomely essential to my life as an anxious traveller: an upset stomach and constant catastrophising about embarrassment, physical illness, death and the general futility of everything.

My maelstrom of dread lasted for three days and three sleepless nights. Although by that stage I was a committed boozer – like almost any other 25-year-old British male in the noughties – I refused the sauce just as I rejected the doctor's offer of beta blockers. I had friends who'd taken them and the side-effects ranged from impotence to nausea to … higher anxiety. They'd also had to up their dosage every few months, which smacked of addiction. I didn't want to trade one portfolio of predicaments for another. So, I waited it out. By day four I was barely functioning, stranded between states. Exhausted but unable to sleep, hungry but with no appetite, needing fresh air yet scared to leave the front door.

That fourth evening my friend Alex brought me valerian root, first used in ancient Greece to cure insomnia. He justified it as a 'natural' remedy far better than the chemicals in mass-produced alcohol or the drugs that my GP was peddling on behalf of Big Pharma. Alex made a tea from the valerian. After three cups, I was snoring in front of a DVD of the war movie *Kelly's Heroes*.

The next morning – or early afternoon – Alex told me something that rallied me in what was shaping up to be a long war against anxiety. He'd lived with the condition for a couple of years and told me not to blanche from aspects of life that could bring fear and panic. 'If you stop going for job interviews, stop socialising, stop taking public transport – all of it will just be harder in the long run,' he said. 'It might seem like the easier option to get a diagnosis and claim sickness benefits, but that's a hole that's hard to dig yourself out of. It'll be a much-diminished life.'

I asked him what he thought caused his anxiety.

'An existential quagmire,' he said. 'I didn't know what to do with myself. I had no purpose, no meaning. Not that I do now, but I'm working on it.'

This was one of the drivers of my funk, hard as it was to admit it to myself, let alone anyone else.

'What do you really want to do with your life?' asked Alex.

'Write, I suppose.'

'You used to want to travel, too.'

'I still do, I suppose.'

I thought about how travel might help, just as even an unambitious form of it – walking from school to my grandmother's house – had helped me become more independent as a kid. This couldn't be some hedonistic holiday, though, after which I came back to an even more alienated and empty existence. If humans should live and work with meaning, love and creativity, as Fromm implored, then I needed to travel in such a way, too. Travel had to be wedded to a more profound project of self-reinvention, it had to lead to a new way of functioning and a new attitude to myself and the world, myself *in* the world.

5

Before I could travel anywhere I needed money. To get money I needed a job. On my next visit to the Jobcentre Plus I tried to be more *proactive*, to invoke an idiom of the era.

'You're a smart chap,' said my employment adviser, a hirsute, ageing metaller. I stared with grim fascination at his soggy locks as they distributed dandruff over his collar. 'You've got a degree, that'll stand you in good stead.' He took a swig of a then-newfangled energy drink called Red Bull.

'Everyone's got a degree nowadays,' I sighed. 'And mine's in twentieth-century American fiction.' I leafed quickly and mockingly through the slips of paper I'd printed up from the job-search computer terminals. 'Not much call for that in the modern labour market.'

'Well, that's society's fault, as far as I'm concerned,' said the advisor. 'I've got a degree in fine art and I never saw myself doing this kind of work. You can't always get what you want, as they say, so the trick is to find something that will keep your mind occupied, at least. What have you got there, mate, out of interest?'

I read the slips in deadpan. 'Accounts Controller. Data Inputter. Catering Services Manager. Abattoir General Operative.'

The advisor clicked his mouse and pushed his nose almost to his PC screen. 'Class 1 Driver: Nights?'

'What's that?'

'Driving lorries at night. Good money.'

'I can't drive.'

'Trainee Plumber?'

'I'm useless with my hands.'

'Teaching Assistant? That's closer to your academic background.'

I say nothing.

'How about Museum Assistant?'

I remain silent.

'Well? You've got an A-Level in history.'

'I'd find that difficult.'

'How come?'

'I …'

'Come on, you can be frank with me, mate.'

'I have anxiety.'

'We all do. Just got to man up, mate.'

'Mine's a diagnosed condition, so I can't deal with anything public-facing.'

The advisor lightly punched my shoulder fraternally. 'Oh, mate, I feel for you. My brother has the same prob—, I mean condition. Where do you see yourself in five years' time?'

'I honestly don't know.' I've always loathed that question.

'What would be your ideal job?'

'Writing.'

'We had something related to that a few months back, a sub-editor for the local paper.' The advisor typed something, wound his mouse wheel. 'Mmm, nothing like that at the moment. I'll tell you what, I'll sign you off this time so you can keep claiming and we can talk about openings in a fortnight's time. Good luck out there, mate.'

I finally found a job doing clerical work. Though I heeded Alex's advice and didn't retreat from social life, I went out a lot less, which meant spending less money, which meant

I was able to save up to travel somewhere. In the meantime, I took my GP's advice and sought counselling. CBT (cognitive behavioural therapy) was all the rage at the time, then-prime minister Gordon Brown claiming it was a magic bullet to get people off benefits and back to work. In my own sessions, I learned techniques that could stem the flow of anxiety before it turned into a deluge. These ranged from breathing in through the nose and out through the mouth, which increases oxygen intake and corrects the shallow breathing many suffer when anxious, to 'grounding' yourself by observing objects or details in a room. My sister Lucy, who was by this time training as a mental health practitioner, explained grounding as 'slowing everything down, slowing our heart rate down and tricking ourselves into thinking that we're calmer than we are. The adrenaline stops pumping so fast and we feel better.' Distracting yourself by focusing on what's around you places you into the moment, so that you're not worrying about the past or, more importantly, the horrific things that might happen to you in the future.

While these methods headed off full-blown panic and returned me to a state of calm quicker than if I hadn't practised them, they did nothing for the underlying causes of my anxiety, which were situational and existential. As the Fromm-influenced psychotherapist Oliver James wrote in his popular book of that time, *The Selfish Capitalist*, CBT simply sent 'the depressed, wounded worker back to work with a false smile sticky-plastered to their face' and couldn't address the social ills of inequality, consumerism and privatisation that depressed and wounded workers in the first place.

At any rate, I soldiered on in my wounding and depressing job and saved enough for a ten-month trip around Asia. Now this would be a test.

6

'Do not let the porters take your bags,' barked Gopal as we rode the escalator past signs warning death for drug trafficking in several languages. I was too freaked out to ask him why I shouldn't. I assumed they might steal the bags or demand an exorbitant tip. Gopal was an Indian guy about my age whom I'd befriended on the plane from Heathrow to Kolkata. This was the first time I'd travelled outside the West, and I was doing my best to channel my anxiety in a productive way. Stay alert, keep moving, 'keep your eyes and your ears open', as Gopal had counselled back on the plane. Coming the other way on the escalator was a turbaned Sikh policeman airily drumming his fingers against the barrel of the assault rifle slung over his shoulder. He gave me a deferential nod.

When we left the airport, bodies were crammed together like seeds in a pomegranate. They made a low, humming, moaning noise. As Gopal and I tried to pass, the crowd tautened and surged towards us, as if we were freshly arrived film stars. Hands reached over heads, but they weren't seeking a magic touch of celebrity, they were after just enough change to buy a meal. I registered toothless, prematurely aged faces. A woman in a headscarf squeezed in front of me. She was bowing low enough that I could see an emaciated baby with a head the size of a light bulb in a sling on her back. The woman glanced up at me and I started. Her cheeks were warped and crinkled like a burnt sheet of plastic. Her nose drooped towards her mouth like wax dribbling down the edge of a lighted candle. Though shaken, I kept looking at her. It seemed heartless not to. She raised a callused hand in a gradual and shaky way that suggested it was hard labour for her. I fished in my pocket, but I only had English money.

Gopal nudged my elbow. 'Neither the time nor the place to be dawdling, Mr Tom.' He led me on a detour around the crowd.

Outside the car park, a man in an Oxford shirt and sporting a Brylcreemed side-parting strutted over to us. 'Taxi?'

I looked at Gopal. He said something to the man in Bengali.

The man looked at me again. 'Rickshaw?'

I shook my head. I was so nervous the words wouldn't come.

'Bus?'

I shook my head again.

'Helicopter?'

Gopal made a brushing gesture and shouted '*Duhro!*' The spiv backed off and Gopal took me to a pummeled Ford India taxi. We wheezed onto a motorway of rusting Ambassador cars, brashly-coloured autorickshaws and trucks with engines salvaged from farm machinery. We almost collided head-on with a nine-year-old on a bicycle.

'Are you still feeling unwell, Mr Tom?' yelled Gopal above the mechanised row.

I winced in the direction of the nine-year-old. My anxiety had come on in the final hour of the flight and I'd used the excuse of an oncoming cold to block Gopal's barrage of questions that had included how much did I earn, could I help him find a place at a British university and did I have a sister he could marry.

We weaved between men in loincloths with muscular limbs and pot bellies pulling rickshaws by hand. Horse-drawn wagons lugged carcasses swarming with flies. Cyclists somehow balanced on their backs drums of milk as big as their own bodies. On Park Street, the buildings smacked of English seafront hotels, but these Kolkatan equivalents were adorned with something you'd never find at the English seaside: the hammer and sickle flag of the communist government of West Bengal.

'You are staring in wonder at something, Mr Tom,' said Gopal. His tongue pointed upwards and worried at his threadbare moustache. 'Or perhaps you are shocked by my home town?'

'N-no, just c-curious.' He was right, of course, I *was* shocked. This was a scale and intensity of noise, crowds, traffic and poverty that I'd never encountered before. Sure, I'd read books and watched documentaries about India, but they hadn't prepared me for this embodied experience, this assailment of all the senses, not just the ones engaged by media.

'H-how far to the hotel, Gopal?'

'Just ten minutes, Mr Tom.'

The unease slid up a gear from a convergence of realisations. *I've left my bloody water bottle on the plane. I didn't change any money at the airport. I don't want to put Gopal out, as he's already been overly kind by accompanying me to my hotel. At the same time, he's kind of annoying and I won't want him around if the fear escalates. How do I get rid of him politely?*

The Hotel Kwality was covered in black stains and power cables fraying along loose bricks. Above my head more cables bowed and looped and entwined with one another like a convoluted trick performed with a yo-yo.

'I must be leaving you now, Mr Tom,' said Gopal, giving me a firm handshake. He climbed back into the taxi and dissolved into the tempest of traffic. While I was grateful for him chaperoning me across Kolkata's hurdles, I was glad he was gone now, as I just wanted to be on my own. Such is the opportunistic and sometimes selfish mien of the anxious traveller.

I saw a naked man lying in a gouge in the pavement. His skin was coated with ashes. *Is he asleep or is he dead?* I asked myself. *If he is dead, did he get that way because of something that happened in the Hotel Kwality?* I looked for a part of the hotel's barbed-wire-wrapped front door to knock on that wouldn't cut my hand to shreds.

A man in a blue suit and glittering buckled shoes threw open the door to reveal a dust-cloaked reception crawling with cockroaches. The man led me into a cubicle with a single barred window and filthy rags stretched over a bench. I sat down on the bench and tried to hold it together. People dead or dying in the street, hungry children, disfigured women, near-fatal driving – I'd never seen anything like it. I had to keep reminding myself why I was putting myself through this. Witnessing the worst of the world would – or should – make me tougher and sharpen my understanding of humanity and of myself. But this was never going to be easy.

On two occasions, I started heading out of the hotel with the intention of flying straight back to the UK. I changed my mind both times. I contemplated the writers I admired who'd been inspired by unforgiving conditions. In *Playing with Water*, a book about living self-sufficiently on a Philippine island, James Hamilton-Paterson turns the point into a rhetorical question: 'Why the undergoing of extremes to see a few things differently?'

'Undergo the extremes,' I muttered. It didn't reassure me. I paced around my room, hoping to wear myself out. I started crying and must have cried myself to sleep, although I don't recall lying down on the rags.

I was woken at dawn by a Black Kite squawking and bashing its wings against the bars of the window. Outside, market traders were yelling '*Eyi-dige aashun! Khub bhalo maal!*' (Meaning 'Come this way! Really good products!', I was later to find out.) Around them the peals of autorickshaw engines grew. From deep within the hotel came the sobbing of old pipes and the gargling of sinks and toilets. It sounded like the digestive workings of a Lovecraftian monster.

I dared not leave this room – squalid as it was – and enter the mayhem outside. If I did, I'd be unable to move for beggars or be run over by any one of a variety of bizarre vehicles. I hated myself for thinking like this, but the anxious traveller doesn't get to choose their thoughts.

7

I persevered on that trip and was rewarded for it. To paraphrase a self-help book of the time, I felt the fear generated by the heat, the smog, the stampedes of beggars, vendors and rickshaws, the dangerously uneven streets, the new and not always hygienically-prepared food – and did it anyway. I guess the fear may have been outbalanced by happy insights gained into a dazzlingly different culture, history, geography and belief system, through visits to temples, fortresses, museums, nature reserves and a cinema where I picked up a lifelong interest in the Indian Parallel Cinema films of Guru Dutt and Satyajit Ray. We can be an adaptable lot, we *homo sapiens*, when we try. And when we change our attitude to something, that something somehow becomes more hospitable to us. 'There is nothing either good or bad, but thinking makes it so,' opined Hamlet.

If the mavens of mindfulness claim that homing in on 'the now' levels your head, I was doing that without meaning to. When I travelled into Southeast Asia, I noticed that most others on the backpackers' trail were doing it, too. The past didn't matter nor any identity formed in it. In each other's eyes we were equal in the sense of all being outsiders, albeit ones way more privileged than the local people we travelled amongst. Amongst us backpackers nobody cared about national background, whether you were British, Canadian, Swedish, Russian or whatnot. Occasionally, Americans got a hard time, this being post-Iraq War. But most Americans enlightened enough to have left America tended to be against American foreign policy. Neither were there usually questions about previous work, education or relationships. Indeed, I got the impression that backpacking, described to me by a likable Devonian also called Tom as 'a really long and expensive holiday', liberated many from the anxieties of having to live a normal, settled life. For now, anyway, I didn't have to worry about building a career, meeting a partner, having children and other such grown-up expectations. In this way 'backpacker' became an identity for some, a reason for being and sometimes aggressively asserted. An infuriating archetype was the hench Aryan bloke from either Germany or one of the Nordic countries who, no matter my own achievements as a traveller, had always trekked further into the jungle, dived around more beguiling shipwrecks, necked more magic mushrooms, etc.

By the same token, no backpackers I ever met talked about the future beyond their next flight or tourist attraction. I never thought about what I'd do when my trip ended nor talked about it with others. There was too much to be preoccupied with in the very short term. My refusal to project forward was also down to a type of generational privilege which young British people don't enjoy now – I knew that when I got home there'd be jobs available, rent would be cheap and the cost of living not barking mad. Indeed, my sister Lucy, in her work with mental health charity MIND, says that today's youth are infested with anxieties about the near and far future. Exam stress has dogged students since the age of abacuses, but the stakes are even higher now with so few decent jobs to look forward to in our age of precarity and automation. And if they decide to stay in education, there's the terror of bankrupting themselves with extortionate tuition fees. Kids are that much more competitive and self-conscious today, no thanks to cyberbullying and online 'comparison culture'. Stuck in the middle of culture wars and fake news storms, they don't know who to trust or what to believe. And their resilience to all this is banjaxed by 'a lot of changes going on in their bodies hormonally,' says Lucy.

On those travels I started to feel lucky, whether the luck was self-made or not. I never fell victim to a con or crime. When I left a pair of shoes on a bus in Thailand, I found they'd been returned to the next station along the route. I started to push that luck, play hotspur. I walked seven miles through downtown Phnomh Penh without being run over or choking on the fumes from burning tarmac. Despite Foreign Office warnings, I journeyed to Indonesia, the most populous Muslim country on earth and allegedly an Al-Qaeda hotbed. I was greeted by warm, humorous and English-football-obsessed people who hated Islamist extremists as much as any Western neocon. While snorkelling off the Gilli Islands, I was sucked out to sea by a powerful rip current and fought my way back to the shore.

I was exposed to new and astonishing scenery. Where I came from there were no jungles, active volcanoes, butter-smooth beaches or thousand-year-old Buddhist shrines. Eternal fine weather allowed activities I'd never tried before: diving; fishing; trekking; sleeping on beaches. Most of the important aspects of Southeast Asian life took place outside: eating; drinking; working; mingling – an obvious contrast to back home. Hailing from an adversarial culture where people yelled across the streets by day and drunkenly fought each other on those same streets by night, I welcomed the Southeast Asian mien of comradeship and hospitality. Each time I got lost or confused on my way, someone helped me with directions or a cold drink or a lift on the back of a motorbike. Visitors to my own country were never treated this well.

I think what kept me chill was sticking to my plan to travel with purpose, to learn and to absorb. There was a point to being here other than pure hedonism. Okay, so there was a bit of hedonism – I was a bloke in my mid-twenties in a milieu of cheap intoxicants and full moon parties. That ten-month-long trip around Asia, which took me to eight countries, was the only time I have kept a daily diary, which would eventually provide material for my first published – and paid for – writing. When you travel there are lots of periods of inactivity. Tedium, lethargy and emptiness can creep in. Writing, recording, observing and socialising stopped that happening to me. Facing off anxiety hasn't always worked like that, but it seemed to for that odyssey in 2007 – or at least until November 2007.

8

In Hanoi, Vietnam, a teenage girl in *Spongebob Squarepants* pyjamas crashed her moped into my right calf. It was one hell of a whack, as the mudguard cracked in half. After initial numbness, pain whisked through my leg like I'd been injected with it. I panicked when I realised that this was the leg that had my birthmark on it. Although benign when I was born, this accumulation of blood vessels under the skin – known as a 'port-wine stain' – had scabbed over by the time I was thirteen. From then on it would start bleeding whenever I played sports and even sometimes when I was sitting still. Just before Christmas 1993, I went into hospital for a skin graft operation which fixed the bleeding for good – or so I was promised. I'd hardly thought about my birthmark until now.

Steeling myself for the worst, I yanked up my trouser leg and was relieved to find that the patch of red – whose shape then resembled the continent of South America – was fine. The teenager put her hand over her mouth and laughed, in what I also assumed to be relief. 'Gorbachev!' she exclaimed.

She wasn't wrong, as that other, marginally more famous birthmark-owner Mikhail Gorbachev had a port-wine stain on his forehead.

My next stop was Kuala Lumpur, Malaysia. Radically different again to both Hanoi and Kolkata, it seemed like a parody – or perhaps the epitome – of Western consumerism. Capital surpluses had been spent on extravagant vanity projects – at that time KL had put up some of the tallest buildings in the world – and hi-tech shopping malls with helter-skelters built into their roofs. But there was something more Western than the West about KL's embrace of Western ways. London and New York were grungey and decrepit compared to KL's Spartan streets and glossily new architecture. Its roads and public transport systems were way faster, more efficient and more logical than their run-down Global Northern counterparts. The hygiene standards of the most primitive food court put any greasy spoon back home to shame.

I went down to Chinatown. It had avoided the globalised blandness of KL's business districts. No skyscrapers or giant video screens here. Arriving at the top of Jalan Sultan Street in a taxi, the headlights fell on a temple decorated with dancing Buddhas and dragons breathing curlicues of fire. Tucked into the shadows of alleys were stalls of Malay and Mandarin comic books, and café windows from which ducks were strung up by their feet. In the gutter, a girl in a sarong swept a torrent of palm oil, fish balls and cigarette butts towards me. Although extinguished, the butts still reeked of clove, the smell preserved in the humid thickness of the air.

As I moseyed, an elderly Tamil woman with a cataract in her left eye offered me some flip-flops.

'No, thanks,' I said.

'No, sir, you buy! You buy! You buy!' she hectored.

Feeling sorry for her, I handed over some coins and put the flip flops on. She looked down to below my shorts and saw my birthmark. Her eyes and mouth burst wide open. 'You are lucky!' she squealed. 'You are Mr Lucky Leg!'

My luck ran out two weeks later in Kuta, Bali's biggest resort, even though earlier on that day it seemed that nothing could go wrong. I got up late after a great night's sleep and showered under the single tap in my room. I lay naked on the bed, meditating on the multi-coloured plasters over the holes in the mosquito net, while the heat dried me off in minutes. Again, this would be impossible to do in England, perhaps fatal during an English winter.

I made my way through the snaky back streets, past women slapping washing against doorsteps and men carving *wayang* shadow puppets. I breakfasted on cheap oysters at a resto-bar oozing the gentle percussions of *gamelan* music. Wherever I went in Bali, this exact same *gamelan* track was playing on a loop. I found the repetition comforting, though.

'Hot today, sir,' said a Balinese-Chinese waiter in a sauce-stained *batik* sarong. 'You want a lucky cola?'

'Sure,' I replied.

The waiter disappeared and I heard the sound of a blender, like a heavy smoker clearing his throat for two minutes. The waiter returned with a glass of muddy-looking cola. I drank it, noting the bitter taste, then headed for the beach.

On the way there, I started to feel as if I were breaking free from myself. I looked down at my arms and legs and they seemed far away, as if my neck had stretched to the height of a tree. I felt like I was ceding physical control over my body in return for heightened visual awareness. Outside the curve-edged pyramid facade of the Ramayana Kuta Hotel, I knelt to look at the paving stones with euphoric curiosity. I saw Balinese characters shaped like petals, eyelids and candy canes. The more I studied them, the more they throbbed and the higher they floated into the air.

Everything on Kuta Beach seemed to be swaying in unison, dancing to the same rhythm: skeletal palm trees, black and yellow parasols, surfboards dug into the sand. There were no sunbathers and, for once, the sea wasn't crammed with Australian surfers. Maybe today everyone was too hungover. I sprinted to the shore and dived into the barrel of a world-class wave. I saw myself from the vantage point of one of the groaning helicopters overhead, watched my hapless frame shoved and slapped about by the water. But I felt nothing.

The last thing I remember from that day is sitting on the beach at nightfall. Spotlights belonging to seafront hotels searched the black sky like the bat signal from the *Batman* films, threading between the smaller, flashing lights of helicopters and planes full of fresh tourists.

A sharp pain in my leg woke me the next morning. I lifted my head and looked around. At least I was in my own bed in my own room. I looked down at my birthmark which had turned into scabs ringed with blood and crowned with amber pus. I was hit by other sudden realisations. The 'lucky cola' I'd been given must have contained psilocybin mushrooms, a legal and widely-available high in Bali. What had I done to myself in that altered state? I checked my pockets and found my wallet and passport.

Shit, I'm an anxiety sufferer, I chided myself. *I shouldn't be taking such substances.* The worry that my drug intake could stir up anxiety was enough to stir up anxiety. My adrenaline spiked, I fought for my breath. I hadn't felt like this in ages. This was a huge step – a long jump – backwards. *Control your breathing. Focus on that mosquito crawling on the other side of the net. See his massive black peepers like Aviator sunglasses. Those hairy, serrated antennae. How much blood does the average mozzy need each day to survive?*

The grounding exercises brought me back to stage one anxiety. I was now well enough to go to a clinic where I joined a queue of surfers with a panorama of injuries from concussion to broken bones. The nurse bandaged my wound and the doctor prescribed me antibiotics, the standard Asian remedy for any illness, so I'd learned on this trip. The doctor said that I needed either laser treatment or a skin graft to prevent blood poisoning and/or possible amputation. My travel insurance wouldn't stretch to such an op. My only choice was to go home.

9

Back in the UK, my GP told me there'd be several weeks' wait to see a skin specialist. At first the cold weather did me good and the wound closed up – I hoped nature had cured me. I started plotting my return to Asia. But then I started bleeding randomly in situations where you don't want to bleed randomly. I'd be sitting in the cinema and suddenly my foot would feel hot and moist inside my shoe. I'd stagger to the toilet to find enough toilet paper to staunch the flow, leaving a trail of bloody bootprints. Other times, I'd be walking down the street, feel a tingling sensation in my calf and look down to find my trouser leg spattered with blood, as if I'd been shot by a sniper.

The specialist got in touch and asked me to go for laser treatment at Salisbury District Hospital. After being introduced to a machine that looked like the offspring of a vacuum cleaner and a dot matrix printer, a male nurse asked me to lie face-down on a leather bed. I felt brief stabs of pain like an elastic band flicking against my leg. The laser failed to delete any of the yellow wound. The specialist advised plastic surgery.

A month later, I awoke in agony in a theatre at the same hospital. The doctors had taken skin from my buttocks and tried to graft it over most of my birthmark. But where there should have been terra firma there was just the bubbling swamp of an infected wound. I gritted my teeth while a laidback Nigerian surgeon took swabs from it. She kept repeating the phrase, 'There there, my sweet, y'all right, y'all right'. Her voice moved at a leisurely tempo and there was a musical quality to the way it would pitch up on and elongate vowel sounds. The surgeon would have been soothing to listen to had it not been the case that nothing infuriates me more than someone trying to tell me I'm fine when I'm in a state of agony. I'd rather they just stayed quiet. Not that I have the courage to tell such people to stay quiet – that would be mean.

'I'm no expert,' I winced as the surgeon rolled the tip of the swab around the wound one last time, 'but this doesn't look better to me.'

'Have to wait and see, dear,' she said, leaning away from me and closing her eyes.

'Is it infected?'

'For now ... yes.'

'It wasn't infected before I came into hospital.'

She patted me on the shoulder and breezed over to the next bed.

Over the next few days, I felt like a guinea pig. I was rigged up to a drip that fed me antibiotics from a transparent IV bag hanging from a stand beside my bed. Junior doctors popped in every couple of hours to take blood samples. They always seemed rushed off their feet. Nurses came to take my pulse and blood pressure and feed me Tramadol pills from little plastic cups the size of shot glasses. Though this drug stopped the pain, it also quashed my appetite and constipated me. Oramorph – a liquid form of morphine – was on offer, too. I confess that sometimes I requested this for the pain while in truth wanting it for the boredom, which is just another form of pain.

'So, when can I leave hospital?' I asked the Nigerian surgeon during her morning rounds.

'Not yet, dear. We need to cure you of this infection.'

'Then what?'

She hesitated. The nurse beside her said, 'Tom, we will need to operate on you again.'

I dreaded the daily bandage change. Knowing the pain that was in store for me, I felt like a man on death row as I waited for the nurses to appear with their equipment. Sometimes it was straight after breakfast, other times it was just before lunch.

I was anxious, as you can imagine, but my restlessness was stifled by my inability to leave my bed. Instead, I had to deal with intense jitters of the mind. I couldn't get three pages into a novel or five minutes into a film. The then-primitive games on my mobile phone offered no respite. I consoled myself with the knowledge that, after the grief of the bandage change, I'd feel a bit better.

The bandage itself was a complex construction of three rolls of crêpe, two brands of antiseptic, a dozen gauzes, a padded outer layer and enough tape to seal up the mouth of an erupting volcano. It was all held in place by a plaster case as heavy as a dumbbell. It took a nurse – sometimes two – at least an hour to get all this unstuck from my wound, causing me such pain that, in my vision, the ceiling of the ward would start to slide in and out of focus, as if I were adjusting the lens of a camera. One time, when a cocktail of Oramorph, Tramadol and paracetamol failed to do its job, the nurses considered putting me under completely. Instead, the addition of Entonox gas, a.k.a. laughing gas, just about pushed me into the comfort zone.

Whenever I had to use a wheelchair to get to the toilet, I felt for the legless beggars on trolleys I'd seen in the poorer parts of Asia. Bed baths were particularly uncomfortable as everything in my little space – from blankets to books to curtains – would get drenched in soapy water. I compared this shtuck I was in to the active life I'd been leading in Asia. In wretched moments, I feared never being able to swim or hike or even walk again. *I'll never leave this place.*

Addiction stopped me heeding the doctors' advice that smoking was disastrous for skin healing. On the second night, ravenous for nicotine, I gave the nurse the excuse that I needed to leave the ward to get a signal on my mobile. I put on my dressing gown and manoeuvred myself into the wheelchair, raising my bad leg up in a stirrup. I then wheeled myself along the lengthy corridor to the lift, travelled down eight storeys to the ground floor and slid out down the ramp to the open air, the automatic door opening just in time for my outstretched leg not to collide with it. I smoked a cigarette at lightning speed, withdrawal aches clearing out from my head and sanguine thoughts entering. *It's not so bad*, I said to myself. *It's not as if my life is in danger and, anyway, I'll be out of here eventually. I bloody well hope.*

As I flung the butt to the ground, I noticed that the ramp seemed unusually long and steep for wheelchair use. I realised it wasn't intended for wheelchairs. Ascending it would be harder work than salvaging Dr Shipman's reputation. I backed up, pressed the green 'open door' button and wheeled myself as fast as I could in order to gain enough acceleration to clear the ramp. Running out of steam halfway up, I rolled pathetically backwards all the way to the smoking shelter. Had I applied the brakes, I might have at least been able to pause and try again from that closer point. I was still a novice in the ways of wheelchair control, though. I tried once more and made even less progress. Eventually, an old gent with an arm in a sling was kind enough to push me inside. He'd been smoking, too, and perhaps had taken pity on a fellow addict.

When I arrived at the ward, the nurse narrowed her eyes and cocked her head. She knew precisely what I'd been up to. Discretion stopped her from saying so.

10

After the doctors' morning rounds I got talking to Aidan, the patient in the neighbouring bed. He was about my age and had been bitten in the face by a Rottweiler belonging to his mum's boyfriend. The police had mistaken him for a burglar and interrogated him for several hours. In that time, he'd developed a nasty infection. It didn't look so bad to me now – just a few grazes and stitches along both cheeks. The surgeon had told him he was fortunate not to have been disfigured.

Opposite us was a teenager, Kev, who'd arrived late last night. He'd put his arm through a window after a pissed-up argument with his girlfriend. Some glass had pierced a vein. He had to hold his bandaged arm above his head at all times.

'Anyone got a fag or a rollie I could scav?' asked Kev.

'Yeah,' Aidan and I said simultaneously.

'Go for a smoke us lot then, yeah?' said Kev. 'Lemme just check if it's all right with the nurse.' He pressed the call button by his bed and a nurse came over. 'I'll ask the doctor,' the nurse said, clocking Kev's bed number. She returned, nodding.

As we headed out of the hospital, we looked like casualties from a war film. Aidan, the most able-bodied of us, pushed my wheelchair while Kev followed behind, his arm held aloft. Outside, I asked Aidan what he did for a living. 'I'm a nurse at Broadmoor.'

'*The* Broadmoor?'

'Yeah, the secure hospital, or prison as most people know it. Although we don't call them prisoners anymore.'

'Do you work with all those famous criminals?'

'Some, like Peter.'

'Peter who?'

'Peter Sutcliffe, the Yorkshire Ripper. He's actually a really nice bloke. Very charming, very friendly. He loves to chat about horse racing. You wouldn't believe he did all that terrible stuff. So, what about you? What do you do for money?'

'I'm a writer of sorts.'

'What do you write about?'

'Asia mostly.'

'Wow, just been out there myself, to India. Amazing. Made me think that, even though I'm technically poor in this country, I'm better off than most of them lot over there.'

'Where did you stay?'

'In Hyderabad, with this Muslim family. The mum was a nice bird. She ran this charity for victims of acid attacks, you know about them, do you?'

'I've seen the effects.'

Aidan pointed to his stitches with the fingers gripping his cigarette. 'It's sort of how I got this. When I come home, I go see my mum and her boyfriend. We have this awful barney. My mum's boyfriend, he's proper BNP. He says to me, "Those Muslims are savages. They're animals for doing that to their women. Thank God we're civilised in this country. We don't want any more of them coming over here."

'So, I say to him, "Violence happens to women here all the time. I work in Broadmoor with the Yorkshire Ripper!" He doesn't like that, but he's thick, he can't argue back. So, he only has his fists, and he's not much good with them neither. He swings at me, misses, then I swing at him, land one on his chin. His dog goes mental, starts barking at me. Barks the whole estate down. My mum's boyfriend shouts, "See him off!" and I get this in the face for my troubles.'

'How did you get arrested?' I ask.

'So, my mum's boyfriend pushes me out the door, rings the police and tells them I'm a burglar. Cheeky bastard.'

From my low position in the wheelchair, I could see under Aidan's legs to the ground behind him. It was rapidly pooling with blood. It took me a moment to say anything. 'Shit,' was what I finally said.

Aidan turned round and there Kev was, staring through the smoke from his cigarette at the claret being decanted from his arm bandage. 'I-I'll get him back to the ward,' Aidan hyperventilated. 'Then I'll come back for you.'

I sat there for half an hour before a nurse, features pinched with disapproval, came to wheel me to the ward. Climbing into bed, I saw doctors and nurses rushing in and out of Kev's closed curtains. 'I just wanna see my family!' he begged in between high-pitched screams. He'd come across as a double-hard geezer twenty minutes ago. I guess we all have limits to our resilience. His screaming went on and on. I couldn't drown it out with my headphones.

I was sliding close to uncontainable fear and about to ask a nurse for help when Kev went suddenly mute. He'd been sedated. Behind the curtain I heard a nurse tut and whisper, 'He's a very lucky young man. He could have bled to death. Looks like we mixed him up with the lad who was in this bed last night.'

I vowed to myself that I'd never smoke again if this was what could happen. Do people need a crisis as a precondition for progress? Can gains ever be made without losses first? Was this a lesson for life in general and did it apply to anxiety, too? I thought about my own situation. It had taken several crises – the failed operation, the wheelchair ramp farce, seeing Kev almost die – to make me get better.

Over the following days, when my body cried out for nicotine, I told it sternly: *You will never leave this place. You will never be free of a wheelchair. You will never travel again.* I forced myself to believe that none of these risks were worth taking for a few minutes of feeling slightly less crap than usual.

11

A tall and muscular skinhead dressed only in a surgical gown took the bed next to Kev's. His right hand was bound in plaster, and both biceps were blazoned with eagle tattoos. He sat silently on the end of the bed and stared at me, his bandaged hand held up in a kind of raised fist salute. I couldn't work out whether his sneering nose and red-glazed eyes were signs of anger or whether they were just his natural expression.

With fearful thoughts of Broadmoor and the nurse's bed muddle fresh in my head, I did everything to avoid the gaze of this mad-looking individual.

Ten minutes later he got up slowly and deliberately, as if his legs were having trouble supporting his considerable frame. He strode over to me, bandaged arm remaining in salute. Without softening his expression, he introduced himself as Jerzy from Poland. He asked me for a cigarette in shattered English: 'I pay back when woman come.'

'Sorry, I've run out,' I said.

'Okay,' he said and wandered out of the ward, barefoot and still wearing only his surgical gown. A few minutes later, a nurse came to his empty bed and asked me where he'd gone.

'He didn't say.'

Jerzy returned two hours later looking slightly more cheerful. He must have found his cigarettes.

On the morning of my op, a fresh supply of casualties entered the ward as I was going nil by mouth. Many of these people had been injured in a steam engine festival. One woman had, like Aidan, been bitten in the face by a dog who had taken a fancy to her Cornish pasty. A man with a drum-sized beard yet no hair on his head had mangled his hand in the spokes of a steam-powered bicycle. I felt guilty – almost every other patient had had some appalling accident whereas I'd ended up here from hanging out in exotic countries.

I lay in bed trying to ignore my throat going dry from lack of water, my belly aching from lack of food, and everywhere else aching from lack of nicotine.

Eventually, two nurses in surgical gear appeared. They told me that my op had been pushed back to this evening. They had to prioritise life-or-death cases over mine.

'Could I at least have a drink of water?' I croaked.

''Fraid not, love.'

Lowering my head back onto the pillow, I started to talk with the bearded man, who introduced himself as Geoff. He was well enough to be able to sit in a chair beside his bed. He was waiting for a consultant to discharge him.

'Bloody mad, isn't it?' Geoff said, shaking his head. 'They made me wait for my op, too, about eight hours in the end.

And this is supposed to be a developed country? I tell you, when I was in the Philippines, I went into a hospital there and, well, it's like a bloody palace compared to here. I told that to the Filipino doc on this ward – what's his name?'

'Dr Ocampo,' I said. 'I haven't met him yet, but I've heard his name.'

Geoff ranted on. 'I said to him, "You've missed a trick coming all the way over here, mate".' Geoff shook his head again and laughed.

Distracted by a sudden, heinous craving for a cigarette, I tuned out of what Geoff said next and tuned back in at this point: '... so they're ahead of us in other ways, too. Like, for example, if you get burgled and the police catch the crim, they'll get your property back for you then give the crim a bloody good hiding. He won't be burgling anyone again in a hurry. That's what they call a deterrent, that is.'

'So, why did you go to the Philippines?' I asked. 'Working there?'

'No, mate,' Geoff winked. 'I went there for the ... attractions ... of the female kind.'

'I see.'

Geoff's head tipped back against his pillow and his eyes glowed. Perhaps he'd lost himself in some pervert's reverie. When he came back to the present, he asked me if I had a fag.

I wished he hadn't mentioned it. 'No, I'm told smoking could ruin my recovery.'

'That's another thing about this hospital,' he said. 'They don't sell fags in any of the shops. Bloody disgrace.'

'Really? Jerzy over there bought some.'

Geoff laughed again. 'Jerzy had to walk an hour into Salisbury to buy some. Nurse said he would have died if he'd started bleeding on the way. But those Eastern Europeans, they're built like brick shithouses, aren't they? They can handle it. I couldn't, mate.'

A kind of tinnitus was building up in my ears, like the seething of a million jungle insects. I suffered a spell of troubled breathing as my lungs cleared themselves out. The tinnitus subsided and I became alert to the smallest details of the hospital – the far-off clang of tweezers against a metal bowl, the squeaking of curtains being opened and closed, the clomping of a female consultant's high heels in the ward next door. *You will never leave this place*, I repeated to myself.

At six that evening, a surgeon doing his best to stifle a yawn came to tell me that my op had been postponed until tomorrow morning. He offered no apology – indeed he seemed irritated with *me* about it.

'Can I have something to drink and eat?' I asked.

'Yes,' he said tersely. 'So long as you're nil by mouth from midnight.'

As he hurried off, Geoff rolled his eyes and said, 'Bet he's off to polish his nine-iron.'

A nurse brought me a cheese sandwich and two packets of Wotsits. After sixteen hours of fasting, the food – plain as it was – couldn't have tasted any better. The other patients were sweet enough to make donations from their own supplies. Jerzy gave me half a Polish sausage that his wife had brought him. Geoff slapped a pack of beef jerky down on my bedside table and winked proudly as if he'd just presented me with an OBE. Aidan bought me a can of Coke from the vending machine. This was selfless of him – he'd had no visitors and was so skint that I'd overheard him accepting a train ticket home paid for by the NHS.

I fell asleep on my back, belly tuberous like a sated hog. I was woken at six by a battalion of doctors and nurses holding clipboards to their chests. They whispered amongst themselves and periodically pointed or nodded at my leg. At no point did they speak to me, which added to the sense of myself as a mere test subject. Being utterly ignored had the effect of making me feel extremely self-conscious – and therefore anxious.

An orderly appeared. He was so tall that his bald head pressed up against the ceiling strip light. He gave me a surgical gown to wear and wheeled me down the corridor. I couldn't concentrate on his small talk because that seething sound was back in my ears and palpitations were ripping through my chest. I also couldn't stop thinking of tabloid scare stories about the NHS: scalpels left inside patients; fatal overdoses of painkillers; superbugs. I'd also read about some new, if rare, scandal about patients being given too little sedative before an operation. These unfortunates feel the indescribable pain of being sawn open, only they aren't conscious enough to signal this fact to the surgeons. The premise of a horror flick if ever there was one.

Arriving in the anaesthetist's room, I was helped onto a steel bench and watched as two masked men injected me with a preliminary sedative. I felt my mood lifting into a happy, dreamy state, like lying in a field of fine-smelling flowers on a summer's day, though perhaps not an English summer's day.

'Whoops,' one of the anaesthetists said.

'Wha-what's up?' I murmured, by now so ecstatic from the opiate that I hardly cared if some error had been made and I was about to go the way of all flesh.

'Nothing, nothing,' the anaesthetist said, eyes smiling above the mask. 'It's just that we should have asked you some questions *before* we gave you the injection.'

'Oh.'

'Can you confirm your name?' His voice sounded distant.

'Err ...'

'Can you confirm your name?'

I barely cared to recall. 'Tom ... Sykes.'

'Date of birth?'

'Ten, ten ...'

'Yes?'

'Seventy-nine.'

'OK, Tom, can you count down from ten?'

My first thought when coming round was how the countdown seemed like it had happened a minute ago, even though in reality I'd spent two hours in theatre.

A stocky nurse with arms like boom lifts scissored off the cast and paused to look at the crêpe. 'Aww,' she burred in Dorsetese. 'Looks like the blood's stuck it to the graft.' She gave me a cup of Oramorph before taking an almighty breath and wrenching at the bandage like it was a heavy-duty door bolt. The Oramorph merged with the remnants of the anaesthetic made me dizzy. Everything bent like a circus mirror: the nurse; the bandage; the bubbling blood; the curtain around us.

The nurse disturbed a vein just above my ankle and blood geysered across her lap. I opened my mouth, but no scream came out.

'Think happy thoughts, love,' said the nurse. 'Think of that nice sunny place you went to on your holidays.' I could only think of a sand fly squatting in a forest of human hair, compound eye greedily to the ground, abdomen filling out red.

An Asian doctor with a pen-line moustache and small round glasses walked over, appearing to me to sway from side to side. 'I am Dr Ocampo,' he said in a low, deferential tone. 'We will see if everything is swell.'

Dr Ocampo knelt down and squinted at my leg. From my angle, I could see what looked like a blood-stained patch of coarse leather. Dr Ocampo picked up my notes and chewed his lip while he read them. 'This is your second operation with us, Mr Tom?' he asked.

'Yes.'

'And remind me how did this problem with your haemangioma birthmark begin?'

'Not sure. It started while I was travelling in Asia.'

'Asia. Did you go to the Philippines?'

'Didn't make it there.'

Dr Ocampo studied me, chewing his lip some more.

'So, can I go home?' I asked. A tear in my eye formed a bubble that exacerbated the circus mirror effect. Dr Ocampo's frame narrowed to the width of a stick and his forehead bulged like a hydrocephalus patient.

'Mr Tom,' said Dr Ocampo. 'The graft hasn't been entirely successful.'

I felt more tears welling.

'But I think with daily bandage changes it could improve.'

'So, I *can* go home?'

'Yes, Mr Tom, you can go home.'

12

I left hospital on crutches and moved into a bedsit in Portsmouth. I didn't get out of bed for weeks, the Tramadol making me sleep for sixteen hours a day. I roused myself only for the nurse visits. The nurses told me that, while the infection had gone, the skin graft hadn't taken yet. They were hoping that the islands of new skin would start to bond together over the raw-steak wound.

My predicament seemed to correspond with the state of the world. The news was full of Britain's obliteration by the greed of bankers and the recklessness of politicians. Unemployment had reached Thatcher-era extremes. A shanty town of Polish immigrants had sprung up outside Peterborough, here in the supposed First World. Whatever the opposite of travel anxiety is, I had an ocean of it in 2008. Maybe let's call it inertia anxiety. It was worse than the Sundays of my childhood because I *literally* couldn't leave my bed, much less my house. The prospect of travelling to the local pub was spine-chillingly bleak, let alone back to Asia.

One night I caught my face in my bedroom mirror and was shocked by what I saw. It was a face – if not a place – of strife Balkanised by thick and prominent wrinkles like well-defended frontiers. My forehead had been partitioned by a line running from my widow's peak down to the bridge of my nose. It was a perfectly ruled straight line like one of the borders drawn up by colonial administrators between what are now troubled North African nations. My lantern chin tapered down in the triangular shape of India, separated by old man's jowls from the Pakistan and Bangladesh of my ruddy cheeks. I didn't look like me. I looked older, uglier, worse in every way.

I crawled into the darkness beneath the duvet. It seemed like the safest place to be. The minutes ticked by. I couldn't bear to get up. In the evening, I heard the synthesised church-bell jangle of my mobile phone. I ignored it, burrowed deeper into my bed. I wasn't even interested in finding out who had called. The doorbell sounded ten minutes or maybe an hour or maybe two hours later. I lodged my head under the pillows.

The next morning bills and credit card offers clunked into the letterbox. I heard more ersatz church bells from my mobile and real-life church bells coming from a wedding somewhere far, far away. People in love. People with a connection. Foolish people with a misplaced faith in their own future and that of humanity.

As the sunlight began to shoot through the gaps in the curtains, I briefly considered feeding myself and then concluded there was no point. I still felt sick and I needed to lose weight anyway. It crossed my mind to take a shower. But why bother when I had no one to impress? I was now so sure that my leg would never heal, what difference to my prognosis would slightly improving my personal hygiene make?

My awareness of the outside world vanished entirely. I stopped hearing the grunts of cars and the snarling of dogs outside. I saw nothing because I hadn't bothered to reach over and turn my lamp on. I couldn't even smell the diabolical *pot pourri* of rotten food, stale blood and dead flesh. Twinges of hunger appeared and, just as quickly, disappeared. My leg was numb to the pain that usually dogged it. My brain was operating at a low level. Barely a thought entered it, and certainly not an abstract or sophisticated one.

I can't recall a tipping point, a Hollywood moment, when it all got so bad it had to get better, but there might have been another day of crippling inertia and then I had to do something, anything. I looked through the diary I'd kept when backpacking. I was reminded of jollier times. Some of the anecdotes and observations were halfway intriguing. I typed some of them up on my laptop.

In the weeks following my discharge from hospital, the pain in my leg reduced. The bandage changes got easier. The visiting nurse let me leave the house with the aid of a cane. Before long the infection was gone and the wound was healing. I was also beginning to get somewhere with my writing.

13

Unlike a lot of writers, I wasn't high-born, privately educated or gifted with media and publishing connections. It was therefore spectacularly foolish of me to try to earn my living with my pen, especially after a couple of years of medical problems. At first, I barely scraped said living. When I was starting there were poorly-paid opportunities to write for the web, particularly SEO (search engine optimised) content. Now much of this stuff – I hesitate to call it writing – is AI-generated, but in the mid-to-late noughties actual human beings were needed to type up flat and forgettable descriptions of products and services, adding in keywords to lure traffic. After half a day of doing this for a brand of antibacterial handwash I was ready to throw in the towel, as it were, and go back to data-inputting. At least I'd once again have paid holidays, a modicum of workers' rights and wouldn't have to do my own accounts. What kept me freelancing was being able to work at home and at my own pace – plus the stubborn belief that I might graduate one day to composing more edifying stuff.

That wouldn't happen for ages. And not until I'd sold out in every conceivable way. My morals went down the loo when I took a gig doing promotional copy for a parasitical payday loan company. My IQ dropped by 50 points when I had to assume the persona of a frat boy called Chad and pen inane remarks about YouTube videos of gerbils appearing to dance to Christina Aguilera songs. My self-respect evaporated when I got scammed by an agent who claimed to represent a New Zealand-based overland holiday company. He promised me £200 for fifty blog posts and disappeared off the face of the internet when it was time to pay. Worked up from a brief given to me by a firm of estate agents in Melbourne, my first book – if you can call it that – was an expat's guide to buying affordable property in the state of Victoria, although I'd rather be mauled by a horde of razor-toothed dancing gerbils than put that on my CV now.

This was an anxious existence. It was the closest I've got to the precarity that young 'uns today abide. I was tense about not having enough money and tense about future chances to make money drying up. I was spending too much time hunched over a screen and too little exercising in fresh air. Working for companies all over the world in different time zones, I had to pull all-nighters to meet deadlines at ungodly hours. This was labour that required me to be comfy in my own company, but there often came a point where I'd been alone so much that

I'd start to forget how to talk to people, make friends, form relationships.

In days of yore – the noughties feel that long ago – one could scrape by on tax credits, and rent, food, beer and all other essentials weren't eye-wateringly expensive. And, most importantly to me, I could call myself a writer, just about, since I met Stephen King's requirements: 'If you wrote something for which someone sent you a check, if you cashed the check and it didn't bounce, and if you then paid the light bill with the money, I consider you talented.' Whenever I felt listless about the topics I was given, I drew comfort from Will Self's remark that writing about things that don't interest you at all is the best way to learn how to write.

When I did finally get into journalism and travel writing, other breeds of anxiety came for me with bared teeth. It was just my luck that I entered the business at its death knell. In the digital age punters didn't want to pay for journalism, so there wasn't enough cash swilling around to pay journalists. Whole titles went to the wall. The Murdoch press – moral garbage since at least 1969 – hacked phones, bribed the police and spied on grieving parents to compete with the even smellier moral garbage of social media. At exactly the moment of the phone hacking scandal I was offered the editorship of a local freesheet newspaper. The two events were unconnected, as far as I know. The freesheet's sole owner, an elderly Mitteleuropean woman, sounded off-puttingly jaded on the phone.

'You can just ask anyone to write for the paper,' she said. 'As long as we have content for each week, we shall be fine.'

While I was certain of the answer to this question, I popped it anyway: 'So there isn't a staff, as such?'

'No money for that. There will be *you*, though. We normally invite members of the community to write updates for us. Doctors, nurses, vicars, police officers, teachers …'

'They do this for free?'

'Yes.'

I pictured spending most of my week hassling overworked public servants for updates on charity fun runs. And then I pictured having a nervous breakdown.

'I'll have to politely decline your kind offer.'

'Is the salary not to your satisfaction? I sent the figure in an email while we were talking.'

'Let me have a look.' The amount was less than my current earnings as a freelancer, which was meagre enough. 'I'll *definitely* have to decline your offer.'

Now I was starting to have my name on my published works, critics would sometimes upbraid me – not literary critics but the repulsive creatures who post in the comments sections of websites. As with having submissions rejected, for a writer the first few times they're publicly savaged is traumatising. It's particularly so if the critic happens to be right and points out infelicities of style or factual inaccuracies. It's less stinging if the critic's full of shit, as you hope that anyone else reading it will think the same and not believe their shit about you being shit. That's rooted in a vain fantasy, though, that any more than one man and his dog will bother to read your work, which often they won't.

A whole other crisis can stew in the gap between your virtual identity as a byline and your real identity as a living, breathing person who is a lot more than a mere line of text that reads 'by Tom Sykes'. At first, I couldn't separate the two, taking any swipe at my work as an assault on my essential worth as a human being. The anguish lurking under this is that people will think that this composition you've produced is the best you're capable of, that you worked your heart out for it, when in actual fact you wrote it quickly and sloppily because the clock was ticking and you needed the dosh. Then I realised that most people who know something about the industry know that writers are under pressure and so each publication is a performance not unlike a live concert or stand-up show – sometimes you bomb, sometimes you pass muster, sometimes you tear the roof off. And even if a reader decides that Tom Sykes, member of the human race, should be demoted to the level of pond scum as a result of the little bit of Tom Sykes' consciousness they have accessed through some hack article he wrote, the reader would have forgotten about that very article within hours, if not minutes. Click on the next hyperlink, order some more dross you don't need from Amazon ... And even if a reader did hold that grudge longer – about which I've catastrophised, too, believe me – what does it really matter? It will have no impact on my life – good, bad or indifferent – whatsoever. I'll almost certainly never meet this person unless they turn out to be an obsessive super-fan. Chance would be a fine thing.

An important disclaimer: I write from the privileged position of being virtually unknown. Famous writers do have their share of harassers who conflate them with the work that they produce. So-called cancel culture has added an extra dimension of anxiety to these proceedings, as readers – and viewers of film and TV – confuse a depiction of something gruesome – rape, murder, racism, misogyny, etc – with support of it from whoever depicted it. Again, there go I but for the grace of being so obscure that I've never fallen victim to this fallacy.

14

I'd been a freelancer for five years when I attended the press trip that convinced me to quit press trips forever. I spent every waking moment of it in some purgatory between anxiety and fury. I had good reason. Six other journalists and I were the guests of a French tourist board and two of the party were intolerable. The first bad portent was a woman introducing herself as *name X* who used to be *name Y*. Clearly, I'm not going to tell you what the real names were, but *name X* sounded typically upper-class while *name Y* sounded very working-class. She'd obviously traded appellations for the social capital. I'll call her Ms Twatface from now on. Ms Twatface complained about everything. She refused to eat the food in the restaurants we were taken to – some of them Michelin-starred – claiming that the fish here was off or the steak there was overcooked. She likened the expensive hotel rooms we were allocated to 'prison cells'. She quarrelled with the driver of our coach about the routes he took despite knowing squat about the highways and byways of Normandy. She childishly provoked our liberal group by declaring that the *Daily Mail* was the 'best newspaper in the world' and that 'all swarthy-looking men' should be detained at airports on suspicion of terrorism.

The other wrecker on this trip – let's dub him Mr Twatface – was not so ill-tempered as Ms but kept cracking lame jokes at the expense of the French in particular and foreigners in general. You, too, must be wondering why someone like that would ever become a travel writer. Time and again he'd scan a menu or a billboard and bellow, 'Well, it's all in foreign!' One evening at a Bayeux bistro, he pushed his *moules marinières* around his bowl and groaned, 'I can't wait to go home and have a nice fry-up.'

Most galling about this diabolical duo was that they wouldn't accept any remedies. When given the option of swapping their *soufflé* or *saucisson* for anything else on the menu, they'd either order something else and spurn that too or sulk that they'd lost their appetite. The Twatfaces didn't want things to be okay. They revelled in conflict and enjoyed making tour guides and waiters uncomfortable. There was a performative, attention-seeking aspect to their carry-on, as they'd raise their voices and ensure the entire venue knew about it. More than once did I fantasise about disembowelling them both with a particularly blunt butter knife.

I and one other, Kyle, a Canadian blogger based in Croatia, tried to challenge the Twatfaces early on. Their response was to accuse us of exactly what they were guilty of, in what Freud called 'projection'. This is where, as the godfather of psychoanalysis put it, 'hostility … is ejected from internal perception into the external world, and thus detached from them [the sufferer] and pushed on to someone else'. Thus, suddenly, it was Kyle and I who were whinging and being rude and making off-colour comments, according to the Twatfaces. This was not a good place for me to be – most anxious travellers naturally believe that it's their fault if someone else behaves twattishly towards them. *Did that question seem nosy? Could that look I gave them be construed as disapproving? Was that reference a bit pretentious/vulgar/highbrow/lowbrow?* It took some reassurance from Kyle, who wasn't an anxious traveller and could therefore be more objective about all this, that it was the Twatfaces being twatty to me, not me being twatty to the Twatfaces.

From then on, I would sit on a coach or stand in a museum silently seething while Ms Twatface berated our put-upon guide and Mr Twatface quipped that his five-year-old granddaughter could paint better than all of the notable French abstract artists put together. I was enduring the agony of the double-bind – if I said nothing then the Twatfaces would continue getting away with their disgraceful ways, yet confronting them would only make them redouble their nonsense and invite them to sling mud in my direction. While at this point in my life I hadn't looked into psychoanalysis much – I'll bore you with that later – I had the inkling that whatever the Twatfaces made out was bugging them about France was not what was really bugging them. What was really bugging them was *them*. And that, in turn, bugged the hell out of everyone else on that press trip.

What to do? This was the question Kyle and I mulled over each night in the hotel bar after our colleagues had gone to bed. Mr and Ms Twatface admitted to retiring early because they were too tight to start paying their own way once the free evening meal and complimentary two drinks had been consumed. On our last evening, Kyle remarked that we were the youngest members of the group by thirty years. 'Maybe this generation of ingrate travel writers will die off soon,' he observed. I'm not sure if he meant it in jest, but it was a potential – if harsh – solution to the problem. If the likes of the Twatfaces were so beyond redemption, so unwilling to do the work on themselves that could make them less frictive towards the world, then maybe they had to become extinct and be superseded by those more at ease with themselves and, well, less twatty.

Kyle went off to bed leaving me to think much too laterally about bloodlines. My pilsner-soaked mind swerved from his remarks about the Twatfaces to the fancy that anxiety could be inherited. According to psychologists Daniel Freeman and Jason Freeman, General Anxiety Disorder 'seems to run in families' but that 'genetic influences … are less significant for GAD than for many other anxiety disorders'. That got me thinking, again woozily, about my own family. My dad's side is full of stoic, well-built, no-nonsense Yorkshiremen and women, many of whom served in the military. But just because they never talked about feeling the fear doesn't mean they didn't feel the fear. My maternal line is a different story. While the mum, aunts and grandmother who brought me up never really used the word 'anxiety', they've always been rather open about their doubts, worries and apprehensions.

I blame myself for one incident of this. In the early eighties, just before I started school, my family relocated to a village in the south of France, partly because my dad is a massive Francophile and partly because there was more chance of getting work labouring or gardening there than in Thatcher's Britain. Small kids pick up foreign languages easily so, aged four, I could speak French as well as I could English. My gran, who was a lot older than four, was getting increasingly anxious about not being able to communicate with the locals.

One morning, she said she wanted to buy some groceries at the shop and asked me how to express this in French. Being the little shit that I was then, I made up a line of nonsense and got her to practise it before going to the shop. Half an hour later, she returned in tears. 'They didn't know what I was saying! They thought I was a madwoman!' Only then did I confess. Far from seeing the funny side, she spent the next fortnight or so feeling ever more alienated from our adoptive community. Gran died in 2003 and it remains a deep regret of mine that I never apologised for royally stitching her up in this way.

15

How anxious was Emil Hollanders when he crossed the English Channel in 1858? From Kempen, now in western Germany, my forefather may have been born too soon and not easterly enough to have suffered in the pogroms. In these grisly rampages, 100,000 Russian and Eastern European Jews were burned, clubbed, shot or stabbed to death by mobs whipped up by demagogues. Armies and police forces were often complicit in the violence. As a subject of the Kingdom of Prussia, Emil would have been used to – and perhaps worn down by – what we'd today call microaggressions. There and then, antisemitism was 'actively preached and spread' in workplaces, schools, universities, social clubs, trade unions and taverns, writes the scholar Daniel Goldhagen.

As I look at Emil's name in the 1861 census, rendered in graceful, zaftig handwriting, I picture him, a boy of twenty, being cold-shouldered on that trip by gentile passengers for his dark complexion and pointy features. If he knew much about Britain, he'd have been nervous about emigrating somewhere that didn't allow Jews to go to university, stand for parliament or become civil servants. He may not have been wanted in his place of origin *or* on the journey from it *or* at his destination.

Maybe I'm over-worrying about my dear ancestor and he had a whale of a time on that voyage – incidentally, he may have spotted fin or sperm whales on the way over. Perhaps he was optimistic about a better life ahead. Many immigrants are – have to be. Like other young Victorian men, he could have seen it all as a big adventure, with fortune, glory and a pretty girl the prizes. He had prospects as a professional clock/watchmaker, a skill that was transferable once he'd settled in Portsmouth. Emil might therefore have laughed at the idea of me, his descendant in a way cushier future, feeling even a pinch of dread while travelling in safety, with no risk of shipwreck or cholera, and no threat of racism or poverty, at my point of departure or arrival.

Another male ancestor on my maternal line relished risky travel, if a hand-me-down anecdote is accurate. Great-grandfather John was a rating on a Royal Naval ship dispatched to Archangel in 1918–19 to try to crush the Russian revolutionaries. The ship docked at a White Sea coastal town. Sent out alone on reconnaissance, John found that the place had been evacuated. With homes and shops deserted, he stole as many valuables as he could carry and returned to the ship. His CO asked if there was anything to report. With jewellery and watches bulging under his uniform, John duly said, 'No, sir.' He must have had a great poker face. Conforming to the worst stereotypes of the Jewish spiv, he apparently made a small fortune from selling these hooky items to colleagues on board and, later, civilians in Portsmouth after demob.

Driving through Cherbourg to the cross-channel ferry port some years later, I see African men on pavements and roundabouts. They're about Emil's age when he'd split for the UK. They look at once listless and frantic, yawning and walking in circles around each other or sitting on benches gazing at their phones while swinging their legs. Their bodies are moving without going anywhere. They're stuck between the place from which they came, to which they can't return after risking their lives to leave it, and two places that don't want them – France now and, if they do traverse the water, England.

Whether you've done anything wrong or not, it's hard for the calmest person not to feel a flicker of fear going through immigration control, wherever in the world you are. The beanie-hatted, puffer-jacketed Police aux Frontières officer holds my passport up to the light and studies it with one eye closed, like a jeweller searching for a cutting error in a gemstone. He lowers the claret-bound document and stares at me, both eyes open. Nobody's passport photo ever looks like them, yet this has never caused me bureaucratic grief before.

He pushes a pen and notepad across the desk. 'Write signature.'

Write my own name. This should be easy. Automatic. Second nature. But not in this state. I got little sleep last night and spent the morning stomping aimlessly around the campsite I'd been staying on with relatives. Already feeling disconnected from myself, now I must undergo these tests of selfhood: Is that picture of me really *me*? Can I prove that *I* am *me* by writing a signature that looks enough like the one in the passport, itself a document designed to prove that, wherever I go in the world, *I* am *me*?

If a passport photo resembles us less as our appearance changes from age, stress and poorly chosen haircuts, does our signature alter over time, too? Even a small divergence between what I write now and what's in my passport could trap me in France on suspicion of illegal emigration, like the Africans earlier. As I shakily hold the pen over the notepad, I consider what else about ourselves changes, and whether these changes are so frequent and extreme that they make us contradictory to the core.

16

People like to believe that they are the same at any time, in any place, acting consistently according to a fixed personality and set of attributes, like a computer-game character. Our culture reveres the consistent, steady, principled. But my anxiety-barraged brain reckons this is rubbish. Doesn't the self shift constantly? Tom who goes down the snooker club might as well be a different person to Tom the lecturer, Tom the uncle to toddler nephews. And within those selves are more discrepancies. Tom the writer is a fairly intelligent life form. He has a high level of knowledge about a few tiny aspects of life. But Tom the writer has also done some epically stupid things. One morning, he fell off his bike into the road, almost to his death, because he got his untied shoelace caught on a pedal. 'You buffoon!' came the quaint admonishment from a passing motorist. He was right, though. And there's a warehouse of more tales of total thick-headedness where that came from. So, overall, am I bright or dim? I've been kind and I've been unkind – more the former than the latter, I hope. I can be forbearing or I can be severely impatient – especially when I'm anxious.

The French psychoanalyst Jacques Lacan argued that this self-uncertainty starts in babyhood, when we first notice our image in the mirror. We're relieved to gain a sense of ourselves as a living entity. But the coherence of the body we see – the head attached to the torso, the knee bone connected to the thigh bone, as the old song goes – is at odds with the lack of control we have over that same body. At that age we can't walk, talk, eat or defecate without help. As we get older and gain more power over ourselves we don't solve this identity crisis, Lacan argues. In fact, it gets worse as we come into conflict with the 'symbolic order': the systems of language, law and social norms to which we try to conform … but we never can since these systems themselves are conflicting and fragmented. This is especially true of language, in which words are never quite able to represent the world, our ideas or our feelings.

'Monsieur?' prompts Beanie-man. 'Write your signature.'

I make a squiggle on the page. It sort of resembles the squiggle in the passport below the picture of some chubby-cheeked, big-nosed, brown-haired, middle-aged man called 'Thomas Sykes'. Beanie-man waves me through, holding me with a wary gaze that screams, 'I'm still not sure who you are.' Well, that makes two of us, mate. I scuttle up the gangway, my hope misplaced that the fear will evaporate after this tense encounter.

Get on a boat in the mid-nineteenth century and there was no shortage of stuff to scare the shit out of you. While there was a renaissance in the industry at this time, with some vessels pioneering on-board entertainment and electric lighting, if you were poor and on a cheap ticket – as Emil must have been – you'd have to sleep on the floor in the chilly, damp, rat-infested hold and provide your own food. If you hadn't brought fruit and veg you could get scurvy. Other diseases were available, from smallpox to measles, which spread easily in cramped conditions.

Even if you hung on to your health you'd be vulnerable to thieves and hustlers, *and* menaces beyond the bulkheads. In 1858 alone, there were 24 shipwrecks in or around the English Channel. I don't like those odds. In one of the more vivid incidents, a storm drove the schooner *Excel* aground at Calais, killing everyone aboard apart from one crew member and the ship's dog. Collisions between boats were alarmingly common, despite all the space there is at sea. I wonder if Emil sat out his twelve-to-fifteen-hour voyage oblivious to all this. Or did he know damn well and drew a frisson from the risk? Or was he quaking with anguish the whole time?

I'm quaking with anguish now in the comparatively deluxe Brittany Ferries restaurant. The five relatives I'm travelling with are huddled ecstatically around one menu. There may as well be a heavenly light shining from the laminated card onto their faces. Normally I'd be as enthusiastic as they are about a starter buffet deal including avocado salad, smoked salmon and king prawns. But I'm bloated already, as if pregnant with an elephant. My throat is arid and my phobia of choking on food is back with a vengeance. 'Wasted on me,' I mutter and exit down the mall-like corridor.

17

Shop windows either side of me pitch the duty-free salmagundi of things that make you smell good (perfume) and things that make you smell bad (cigarettes and alcohol), not to say things that are over- and under-sized: irresponsibly large chocolate bars and bottles of whisky, heavily scaled-down models of the ferry we're riding on, minuscule wireless earphones that the manufacturers surely bank on their customers to lose and then have to buy another pair and then another pair and then another pair and so on.

I avert my eyes. I can't take any more dissonance.

As I march – and the distance feels infinite – the kinetic component of my anxiety gears down. My heart rate stalls. I can swallow again. But I'm not out of the scary folk tale woods yet. My head's stuck in a miasma, equal parts futility and redundancy. What's the point of duty-free nowadays anyway? You can get a lower-priced bottle of gin or Bailey's in any supermarket, on or offline. And, in Austerity Albion, there are enough dodgy geezers on street corners selling nicked or pirated baccy, Tommy Hilfiger cologne and, if you keep your voice down and know the code word, a veritable pharaoh's tomb of crunchy caramel M&Ms.

I almost bump head-first into a bloke wearing a slime-green corduroy cap and Garibaldi beard flecked with what could be Garibaldi biscuit crumbs. We both take enough last-minute evasive action to side-step, skim each other's shoulder and avoid injury. I blame my crapper-than-usual spatial awareness on my rattled state. What's his excuse? As I back off, I work it out. He's failed to master his wireless earphones and is listening to the BBC

Radio 4 shipping forecast at a volume that would make a Who concert sound like a provincial library. With 'DOVER, WIGHT, PORTLAND, PLYMOUTH, FOUR TO FIVE, INCREASING SIX SOON, RAIN OR SLIGHT DRIZZLE, GOOD' booming in his ears, he enters a shop to amass his legal maximum of 42 litres of duty-free beer. Actually – and I know we shouldn't judge people on appearances – I bet he's a cider drinker.

The shipping forecast has been aired since 1924, though nowadays isn't much use to actual ships. More accurate data's available online and via satellite. But the forecast remains a 'soothing presence', as an article in *The Week* puts it, for many Britons as they drift off to sleep at night or come to in the morning. Supposing you listen at a reasonable volume, the arresting place names – Trafalgar, Viking, Irish Sea, German Bight – delivered in dulcet RP take the listener on a psychical odyssey of the British Isles. It's been known to trigger ASMR (autonomous sensory meridian response), a gratifying tingle in the head, neck and/or spine. YouTube has oodles of such material – including a twelve-hour compilation of shipping forecasts with a crashing-wave backing track – and there are now live ASMR lounges where you can relax to people right next to you brushing their hair and scrunching up bits of paper. ASMR is not a bad strategy for loosening some of the knots in our anxiety-snarled society. I wish I'd booked a cabin on this ferry where I could chill out to talk of a westerly gale force 6 expected later in Cromarty.

I doubt there were many ASMR opportunities open to Emil on his channel crossing. Simply not getting dysentery would have been cause for sensual ecstasy. Like the shipping forecast and duty-free shopping of our time, the Britain he was coming to had its fair share of pointless and outdated traits. As a lad of limited means he might have been shocked at the money wasted on follies, those mock-medieval, -Gothic or -Ancient Egyptian buildings that sometimes collapsed from their top-heavy towers and over-elaborate features. Coming from mainland Europe where recent revolutions had sent monarchs packing and given new rights and freedoms to the downtrodden, would he have been puzzled by the ossified aristocracy of Britain, whose eccentric titles, customs and costumes must have seemed ridiculous amid a rapidly urbanising and industrialising society?

Travelling presents you not only with things that have outlived their use, but with words and phrases that no longer relate to the things they hope to describe. I see a row of guidebooks in the newsagent: *France, United Kingdom, Europe on a Shoestring*. I don't expect to see my own piddling contribution to the canon, the world's only English-language guidebook to Ivory Coast, but I think of it anyway. 'Ivory Coast' is a misnomer, since no ivory has been available there since about 1800 AD when Europeans wiped out all the elephants. Equally, the nickname of their football team, *Les Éléphants*, is outmoded – but no one cares because they're so successful on the pitch. Closer to home, Warwick University has never been in Warwick, always on the fringes of Coventry. In my hometown, many are adamant that they live in Southsea rather than Portsmouth, even when they are half a mile on the Portsmouth side of the informal border between the two places. Snobbery might drive these mislabellings. Better for your social capital to have graduated from posher-sounding Warwick and better for your financial capital to own a house in Southsea.

As we dock in Portsmouth Harbour, I hang back from the flood of passengers down to the car deck. I can't cope with getting snagged in a tight crowd. I close my eyes, take measured breaths and listen to the gong-like footsteps against steel stairs. These sounds are soon harmonised – though not pleasantly – by church bells from inland. There's another symbol of defunctness, since almost nobody goes to church these days, at least compared to Emil's time. But, like the shipping forecast, there's something reassuring about listening to them. On a hazardous trip such as the one Emil took, it must have been a relief to hear proof that land was near and that, from then on, the risk of getting shipwrecked or falling overboard would be rapidly diminishing. For me, here, seventeen decades later, it's about knowing that, if my unease becomes unbearable and I need to seek help, I'm back home where I know the ways things are done, even if they're not done very well a lot of the time.

Emil didn't have that luxury alighting at Portsmouth in 1858. That said, immigration processes were simpler in his day. Minimal paperwork was involved, as few records of arrivals were kept and you wouldn't need a passport to enter the UK until the First World War. Emil wouldn't have been interrogated unless he was coming from somewhere disease-ravaged. If he was, he might have been checked over by a doctor, but this wasn't very common either.

18

My own more recent experience of trying to get into the UK is more challenging – and I'm not an immigrant. Once off the ferry, we join a funeral train of vehicles that moves slower than a snail ordered down a salt mine. My relative grouses about post-Brexit IT and admin glitches. Just as we're about to pass through the barrier to freedom, an official in a hi-vis vest and a key-shaped piercing through his nose takes a distressingly long time over my passport.

'You have a stamp in here from Tunisia.'

'Yes,' I say, but not loud enough because I'm short of breath.

'What?'

'Yes!'

'And from Côte d'Ivoire. Why were you there?'

'Côte d'Ivoire or Tunisia?' I shouldn't have said that. Might come over as trying to be clever.

'Either.' The official shrugs. 'Both.'

'I'm a journalist.'

His eyebrows leap. 'What sort of journalist?'

'Travel writing mostly.'

'Who do you write for?'

Why the inquisition? I wonder. *Security concerns post-Brexit? Post-refugee crisis? Post-common sense?* I'm so tempted to be snide. That'd be a bad move and my relatives would rightly crucify me for squandering their time. 'Magazines and websites,' I say.

'Which ones?'

'*Travel Africa, New African*, airline magazines.' This line of questioning feels more like a job interview than a probe into whether I've come to overthrow the government of Theresa May – who's doing a strikingly good job of it herself.

'Have you got some ID?'

I nod to my passport still in his hand.

'Some proof that you're a journalist?'

I've barely removed my NUJ press card from my wallet before the official blinks and tips his head back. I guess this means he doesn't need to inspect it. *So why ask for it in the first place? Why ask me any of these questions?* Then I get it. He's asking them not because he's following any particular rules. He's asking because he can, because it's a way of establishing his superiority over me. The urge behind this, again, has nothing to do with who I am or whatever I say to him, but everything to do with his own inner story, his own trauma or anxiety. That's what the psychoanalysts would say. Maybe he was bullied as a child and never wishes to feel that small again, so he grew to be a bully himself and made sure he was always on the side of authority. Was that why he went for this job in the first place, since it can't be that rewarding in other ways?

When the official gets bored of grilling me and the barrier creaks open, I speculate about what hostility Emil, as a Jew trying to integrate into a new gentile society, copped from repressed white Victorians who'd have done well to address the wars within themselves before waging them on others. Records show that he married a woman called Fanny, who belonged to another Jewish family already settled in Portsmouth. How did Fanny's suitors react to this swarthy outsider winning her hand? What did his success reveal to them about their own insecurities? At this time, Portsmouth had the fourth largest Jewish population of any city in the UK and was a hotbed of civil rights activism that lobbied for the Chosen People to earn a degree and go into politics, if they so chose. That would have got some people's backs up. They might also have envied a newly-arrived immigrant who was able to make a living and support a family from crafting timepieces in a land of widespread poverty and joblessness.

Emil passed down his trade to his son, who was also called Emil. In 1886, in what may have been a racially motivated incident, Emil Jr was wrongly accused of purchasing a stolen Jacot tool, a watchmaker's pivoting lathe. This appeared in the local paper, which later the same year would report on a happier event for Emil Jr: his patenting of 'an improved electric safety pistol for firing cannons and explosives'. Chillingly, Emil Jr, Emil Sr and Fanny all died in 1906. I can't find out whether they died at exactly the same time and/or of the same cause. We can rule out a fire or a triple homicide as these would have made the headlines. Their fate remains a puzzle and a source of ancestral anxiety for me, given the time and emotion I've invested in reconstructing my forebears' stories.

And the idea of inherited anxiety continues to weigh on me. Certainly, relatives who are alive today have fought similar battles to me, if not in the travel context. One of the reasons my sister Lucy started working with young people with mental health issues was that she suffered from anxiety at school and college. I have cousins who have been overwhelmed by challenges ranging from starting a new job to having children. As the experts suggest, genetics could be one of multiple origins of our malaise.

PART 3. MY BIG FAT TERRIFYING NIGERIAN WEDDING

1

My Philippines foray confirmed that travel anxiety can clobber me whether I'm in company or alone. But it also showed that certain people who give a shit can talk me down from the fear. In that case it was medical professionals, bless them, and there are others that anxiety-sufferers have access to – if they're fortunate – from parents to close friends. Some folks are just exceptionally calm about stuff and have the superpower of being able to spread it to others. It can be a skill that's honed professionally, as with horse whisperers and hostage negotiators. Others just seem to be born that way – although certain greybeards would argue that nobody is ever 100 per cent free of anxiety, however cool they come over.

I meet someone who has a soothing effect on me. I'm browsing a dating website when I see a photo of a beautiful African woman in a puffed-hand blouse. She's called Oge. Her camera-stare suggests kindness, grace and a confidence that borders on conviction and is perhaps only a few miles from uncompromising. I'm drawn into the swirling patterns on her clothing. They remind me of a lava lamp and the puffed hands – actually on her biceps, technically – are like psychedelic arm bands. Without having met this person, I have the intuition that they're good and that they'll be good for me. If you've done online dating you'll know that it's riddled with fraudsters and harassers. This woman doesn't strike me as either, although, again, I can only guess that at this stage.

I click on her details and find that she's studying tourism. She's created a comely website for a nascent business offering bespoke tours of her native Nigeria. So, we have travel in common, that's good. I'm sure there'll be other things.

I drop her a message through the site. It's never easy to kick off these chats so I say that I've been to other parts of West Africa. She asks me what I liked about them. Music, food, palm wine and animism, I reply. She says that's a strange mix and that her grandmother was an animist before converting to Christianity in old age. She's been in the UK for two years. Does she like it? I ask. She gives an evasive yes-and-no-type answer.

We graduate to chats on the phone. I conclude that if I were to look up the words 'resilience', 'fortitude' and 'forbearance' in the thesaurus, 'Oge' would be a synonym. She grew up in a village in eastern Nigeria that required the proverbial five-mile walk to the nearest source of potable water. She'd survived a public school modelled on the British system and sadistic military training à la *Full Metal Jacket* as part of her national service.

Her sense of humour can be harsh, but it punches up not down. Corrupt politicians and narcissistic celebs come in for the most stick, especially if they're from Nigeria, whose culture and politics she knows intimately. I'm educated about everything from the brutality of the SARS (Special Anti-Robbery Squad), whose killings of peaceful protesters happened around the same time as the US police murders of George Floyd and Dion Johnson, to the yahoo cults that ran riot around her university. A gifted storyteller, she relates in unsettling detail the fear she felt when one of her final exams was interrupted by the sound of automatic gunfire elsewhere on the campus. She's a proud Igbo, I learn, and active in her people's century-old struggle for independence.

In return, I tell her about places I'm passionate about such as India and the Philippines. She's eager to visit them. We'll visit them together, I suggest.

2

After a few months of dating, I consider telling Oge about my anxiety. And then I get anxious about it. What if she resents my only telling her now that we're an item, which will make it harder for her to break up with me, morally speaking? Or what if she freaks out for the opposite reason, demands to know why I didn't tell her sooner? Then, during a meal at her new favourite Thai restaurant in Portsmouth, I'm given a good reason to remain a coward for a little longer.

After a mouthful of beef massaman, Oge says, 'My Nigerian girlfriends are scared to date Western men, *O*.' I've learned from Oge that in Nigerian English you add '*O*' to the end of your proposition for emphasis.

'Scared? Why?'

'They say that Western men have two problems.'

'Only two?'

'One: they have mental health issues.'

'Right. Is that such a bad thing?'

'Two: they are not very good in the bedroom.'

'Are you trying to tell me something, sweetheart?'

Oge howls toothily.

That night I sleep badly from brooding about how heavy a 'mental problem' has to be for these 'Nigerian girlfriends' of Oge's. If I try to explain how anxiety affects me, she might dump me on grounds of irredeemable flakiness. Some women appreciate men opening up about their feelings in this way. I don't think Oge is one of them.

A week later, I spy my opening. We're on the phone when she tells me about the care work she was doing during the Covid lockdown. One day, while she was making a cup of tea for the disabled person she was looking after, she suddenly became frantic. 'I was trembling and felt faint. I did not feel like myself.'

'Why do you think it happened?'

'I do not know. It was a strange time, *abi*.' (*Abi* means 'right' or 'is that it?')

'It was strange for us all.'

'I was supposed to be working in a hotel for my study placement and, all of a sudden, we had no guests. I had to study online only. I ran out of money and had to use a food bank. Strange time in a strange place.'

'England felt stranger than when you arrived?'

'Yes. Even less friendly. People had no time for each other. I was caring for people but no one was caring for me.'

This is quite the turn-up. Until now I wouldn't have believed that Oge has had a single spasm of anxiety in her life – and surely not travel anxiety. I tell her about my own tussles but keep it vague.

When I'm done, she asks almost nonchalantly, 'Have you tried counselling?'

'I have in the past, with mixed results.'

'Why?'

'I either didn't connect with the counsellor or …'

'Or what?'

I don't want to say the next thing – it would seem nuts to Oge. She is as steadfast and sensible as I am erratic and impatient. Maybe we subconsciously seek partners who'll compensate for our own shortcomings – and save us from them, if need be.

'Go on, dear.'

'I didn't carry on with the techniques and exercises the counsellor taught me. You're supposed to do that after the sessions end.'

'Why not?'

'Because I'm lazy.'

'But you are not lazy. You work very hard, publishing books, teaching students, etcetera.'

'Do you know that Chinese proverb about every person having their ration of good luck as they go through life?'

'No.'

'Maybe everyone has their limited share of discipline.'

'And you spent all yours on publishing books and teaching students, so there is nothing left for making sure you, what, keep a diary of all the times you feel nervous?'

Her mocking laughter is justified. My excuse is lame. I am at least shamed into getting more counselling. Oge and I are likely to travel together soon and I don't want to bug her with a meltdown.

3

I find Jacqueline in a flint-grey, semi-permanent structure that looks like a North Korean prison camp. Somehow it has qualified for the ascription 'community centre'. Jacqueline's unit is festooned with new age trinkets and framed 'inspirational' homilies: 'Each day provides its own gifts'; 'If you love life, life will love you back'; 'Sometimes you win, sometimes you learn'.

In the thick of all this, Jacqueline spins round in a gondola-shaped chair to face me. I'm startled, step back and tonk the back of my head against a low-hanging amethyst globe. Jacqueline's not so old but she's pale and tight-skinned enough that I can see her facial bones. She wears a woodcarved rune amulet round her neck and the rest of her – apart from overflowing cleavage – fits into a hooded paisley gown. Her hair is dyed equal parts pink, purple and yellow – a trippy tricolour.

She offers me a cup of rosehip and fennel tea. She asks me what the matter is in a voice that will come to drive me to distraction because it always sounds like a kindergarten teacher addressing her least able student.

I cite my recent travel anxiety and how I want to avoid it in future.

'Tom, do you know something that works really, really well, yes? Breathing in through your nose and out through your mouth.' She proclaims this as if it's the most significant revelation since the Epstein Files. I'm inclined to tell her, in the same condescending voice, all about this law of gravity thing she may not have heard of and that this Donald Trump chap is a malignant narcissist.

Instead, I say, 'I was hoping to get into what causes the anxiety.'

Jacqueline picks up a skull – not a real one but an ornament covered in line drawings of hearts, stars and crescent moons. 'Did you know that in West African animism the skull is the seat of the soul, yes?'

'Er, no, I didn't.'

'Why would you?'

Because I'm thick as eight short planks? I feel like saying.

'I believe that anxiety comes from the soul, yes? We all carry it with us wherever we go and whatever we do. The way we can reduce anxiety is to be kinder to our soul, yes?'

'How can we be kinder to our soul?'

She puts the skull down. 'Have you had any bereavements in the last few years?'

'A couple.'

'Tell me about them, yes?'

I start talking about the deaths of John and Gareth. My throat and jaw ache. I can feel tears germinating from my eyeballs.

Jacqueline extends a hand to me, palm-down, and wobbles it at the wrist. 'Now, now,' she says. 'I think the lesson here, Tom, is that we don't know how much we value someone until they're gone, yes?'

I start to form some more words in agreement, but Jacqueline interrupts again. 'Let's not go there right now, yes?'

'I-I thought the whole point was to go there,' I sniffle.

When I recount this lamentable 'therapy session' to Oge, she says, rightly, 'That is total madness, O. The lady should have let you speak your mind or what is the point of it all? Why distract you from the real issue?'

It seems we share a curiosity about distraction and repression, at least when it comes to emotional matters. Like me, Oge has spent a lot of her time on this planet second-guessing the motives of that odd species known as humanity.

Something else we have in common is a wariness of group mentalities. 'Not being clubbable,' was what my dad used to call it. As a fairly new immigrant to the UK, Oge is aware of the Nigerian diaspora here but isn't automatically keen to be part of it. By the same token, when I was living in Manila, absolutely the last bloody people I wanted to hang out with were other Britons, not least because I knew what kinds of Britons they were – sex pests and reactionaries, often enough.

One Sunday afternoon, Oge comes home in a huff after attending a lunch given by Nigerian members of her Catholic church. 'They did not give me enough food,' she hisses.

'Couldn't you have asked for more? I can make you a sandwich now, if you like.'

'That is not the point. The point is, I queued up like everyone else, but almost everyone else got more jollof rice and chicken stew than me. I will tell you what that was really about: they gave me less food because they see me as a newcomer and lower down in their silly pecking order.'

'Maybe it was just an accident, love.'

'There are no accidents, just agendas.'

4

Slavoj Žižek, whose shivery nervous energy, Marmite-thick accent and rash provocations make him the essence of the eccentric intellectual, tells the story of a German antisemite in the 1930s who has a Jewish neighbour, 'a good man to chat with in the evenings, whose children play with his'. The neighbour defies the stereotypes that the antisemite deals in: the Jew as exploiter, 'wire-puller', sexual predator. But rather than ditch his bigotry in light of the new evidence, the antisemite concludes that Jews must be *more* sinister than previously thought since 'it is exactly this hiding of one's real nature, this duplicity, that is a basic feature of the Jewish nature'. This, for Žižek, is because 'An ideology really succeeds when even the facts which at first contradict it start to function as arguments in its favour.' The stronger the evidence against the belief, the stronger the belief grows, with all anomalies absorbed.

Thirties antisemitism didn't give a toss about the facts on the Jews because its demonisation of them was 'a way to stitch up the inconsistency of our [Nazi Germany's] own ideological system'. Hating minorities is what happens when individuals and societies fail to resolve their 'deadlock of desire' – an idea Žižek adapts from Jacques Lacan – when unconscious needs are unfulfilled or contradictions unresolved. Rather than trying to fix your psyche or your social set-up, it's easier to project your frustrations – and anxieties – onto someone or something else.

My experience echoes Žižek's fable one day outside the Portsmouth Guildhall. Oge and I are attending a demonstration against a gathering of far-right activists. The professional fash are easy to spot. The bomber- or parka-jacketed, tattoo-drenched skinhead archetype has been around since the 1970s. But these guys are outnumbered by people who look like, well, normal people, with problems. People on crutches. With walking sticks. In mobility scooters. With hearing aids. No one's wearing fancy clothes or jewellery. I guess most are working class or unable to work.

These are all clues that their angst has little to do with the signs and flags they're wrapped in or clutching, which are anyway confused. Slogans accuse the 'woke establishment' of fascism *and* communism. 'Billionaires' and 'elites' come in for stick, yet their opponents, like 'liberals' and 'socialists', are equally despised. Some of the skins are wearing Star of David T-shirts, though they probably also deny the Holocaust. How many of them could point to Israel or Palestine on a map? But more unhinged than any of the above is the allegation that Sir Keir Starmer is a 'pinko parasite'. Well, the second half of the sentiment is right.

One doesn't have to be a Parisian clinician or a Slovenian savant to work out what's really eating these people. Poor housing, healthcare, education, jobs (or no job at all). I wonder how many people standing on my side of the divide come from the same background as the people we're shouting at. I grew up in a single-parent family on benefits. At school I was entitled to state-funded 'free dinners' – nowadays the social circles I move in would call them 'lunches'. I had my share of humiliation. I'm still scarred by the stresses of relative poverty. But I didn't end up trying to set fire to a hotel full of asylum seekers or wave a piece of cardboard reading: 'Stop China vaccine genocyde save R kids stop imigrants [sic]'.

Can similar backgrounds and experiences defuse aggro between them and us? Not according to Žižek's logic. Until that old deadlock of desire is broken and someone feels less anxious about lack of cash or prospects, they're only going to harden their hatred for the Jews, the Muslims, the New World Order, Bill Gates or the late actor-musician Kris Kristofferson (whom wingnut conspiracy theorist David Icke unfairly placed into the pantheon of elite reptilian shapeshifters). Shouting across a city centre in the hope of changing these folks' minds will be about as effective as trying to take the Great Old One down with paper aeroplanes. Would you change your mind about something, anything, if someone informs you, even politely, that you are stupid and obnoxious? There you go.

What Hillary Clinton unwisely called 'the deplorables' might also baulk at the hypocrisy in left and liberal gripes about them. Framing the far right as racist, anti-immigrant and authoritarian is never going to land if these same people can point to powerful liberals with similar attitudes and policies. For time immemorial British governments – who would not generally describe themselves as racist or extremist – have cracked down on migrants, censored and sometimes imprisoned peaceful activists, supported apartheid regimes such as Israel and South Africa, prosecuted illegal wars against Black and brown people, and have been four square behind all the functions of the state that are institutionally racist: justice; policing; housing; education; employment. When you look more closely, the antagonism between the centrist and the rightist on these questions belies a lot of agreement, tough as this is for either side to admit. It's a case of what Freud dubbed 'the narcissism of small differences' back in 1917, which was updated and given a political spin by the journalist Christopher Hitchens in 2010: 'In numerous cases of apparently ethno-nationalist conflict, the deepest hatreds are manifested between people who—to most outward appearances—exhibit very few significant distinctions.'

I might sound coolly analytical about all this now, but I've made many of the above mistakes in dealing with hostile others in travel situations. That encounter at Portsmouth ferry port where I hung onto my patience is as rare as any show of humility from JD Vance.

5

If one point in time and space could be said to represent a panic attack it would be Murtala Muhammad International Airport, Lagos, here, now, in late 2022. When we arrive, Oge and I join a mammoth queue in the boarding tunnel. The squat but forceful-looking old woman in front of me squeals, 'You steal my place, O!' at a young mum with toddlers in tow. The mum shrugs. 'Godforsaken country,' Oge says under her breath.

As we pass the toilets, we're forced into separate lines – Oge into one for Nigerian nationals, me in a longer one for foreigners. Everyone apart from me wears a neck pillow like an Elizabethan ruff and carries a see-through bag of duty-free goodies.

The queue divides yet again into those needing a visa on arrival and those having to fill out Covid-related forms. I don't fall into either category, as I already have my visa and my printout proving I've met Covid regs. I'm advised by a man in a hi-vis vest to join the 'visa on arrival' line. When I reach one of the desks along the way, another hi-vis vest inspects my passport and tells me to switch to the other queue.

'That can't be right,' I protest.

He points to a sign that reads 'We do not condone excitation'. I'm trying – really trying – not to get excited.

At another desk by the other queue, another hi-vis vest doesn't want to see my Covid paperwork. He nods at the visa page in my passport and lets me into an even lengthier queue for immigration. I can't see the end of it; I'll be here for hours. More slanging matches break out between larger groups of travellers at various stages of the queue, which snakes all around the arrivals hall. A staff member in military epaulettes and a club tie is heckled by one of the travellers: 'Was my gift not large enough, brother?' Oge will later inform me that bribery speeds the arrival process. If I had cash on me and knew how to distribute it without getting anyone in trouble, I'd hand over a hundred quid to expedite this torturous wait.

I do my breathing exercises. I focus on the steel latticework beams on the arrival hall's ceiling. I thumb my phone, trying to guess the password for the airport wifi even though it isn't open to the public. A futile activity that'll distract me just enough. That it could bring a flow state is asking way too much.

I have to hold it together. There's no option to bail out, call for help. This is international no-man's land. A false move could be taken as cover for drug smuggling or illegal emigration. *If I feel shit now, think how much worse it'll be languishing in a Lagos gaol or getting packed off on the first flight home, my big fat Nigerian wedding cancelled.*

An hour later, when I'm a tantalising fifty yards from the immigration counters, there's another altercation. Like football fans outraged by a refereeing decision, the entire row of arrivals behind me yell and wag their fingers at a swarm of women in natty gold jumpsuits who seem to have come from nowhere to occupy the counters, handing their passports over and posing for mugshots. The rage is infectious – men in Muslim prayer caps break from their rank, further behind, to remonstrate with a bamboozled-looking teenage policeman. For a moment, the serried, half-mile-long queue is in danger of disintegrating. Amidst the chaos, the small, mean-looking woman from earlier bounds through one of the counters without showing her passport. 'This is nonsense!' she shouts behind her, Mr Epaulettes calling after her, 'Madam! You cannot just enter the country like this.' I admire her chutzpah. She got any spare for me?

I enter the zone of tolerable anxiety after I pass immigration – again, without Covid papers glanced at – and go into baggage collection. I'm here sooner than Oge so I gather our suitcases from the carousel and dump them on a trolley.

Mr Epaulettes sidles up to me with a grimace. 'Sir, you cannot leave this here.'

'Leave what where?'

He points at my luggage. 'You are obstructing the door to the toilets.'

I point at the door, which is twenty feet away. 'That door? How can I be–'

'Move it this instant, sir!'

'Where to?'

He waves his hands vigorously like a boy scout fanning a feeble fire he's made with a flint and fluff.

I release the break on the trolley and move it a few inches deeper into the room. 'Better?'

'No, no, sir. More inside.'

I move it another few inches.

'More inside, sir!'

'What the hell difference will it make?' I snap. But what am I doing? Why am I arguing? Because I don't want to let this despot get away with bullying me.

'Do not defy me, sir. You want me to call the policeman?'

'I imagine the policeman has bigger fish to fry.'

Mr Epaulettes plucks a walkie-talkie from his belt. 'Do you want me to find out, sir?'

If this muppet's expecting a bribe, he has another thing coming. I'm tempted to call his bluff, but I do something worse. 'What is your problem? What is this *really* about?'

Mr Epaulettes stares at me sorrowfully and says nothing. He steps back. Now *I* feel like the oppressor. Mr Epaulettes turns on his heel and goes and pesters someone else.

To what extent are people from my part of the world to blame for Mr Epaulettes' rigidity and vindictiveness? On the plane I've been reading *West African Interlude*, a memoir by Richard Terrell of his time as a British official in Nigeria in the 1950s. He describes as 'vital humiliation' the ways in which the colonial regime treated its African underlings. This made them afraid to make 'suggestions for action' which caused administrative 'inefficiency'. All written work in his office was in English, which was taught badly in Nigerian schools. Was this a strategy to pacify the natives and head off more upstarts like Gandhi, who'd mastered their bosses' modes of thought and led independence movements?

6

Calling out the officious almost never works, as we've seen. I once encountered a refreshingly different approach and it *almost* changed my mind about things that I thought I was sure of. In a bar in Washington, DC, I got chatting to a woman whose compact posture and twitching nose reminded me of a chipmunk. She had a mighty Southern twang to her voice like a country and western guitarist bending a low note. I have to confess that, as a Limey brought up on redneck-trashing movies like *Deliverance* and *The Texas Chainsaw Massacre*, I associated such an accent with crassness and idiocy. But this woman – let's run with the stereotype and call her Arlene – was anything but. She was a college professor of economics, had published academic papers and formerly worked in overseas development.

However, she was also convinced of every next-level conspiracy theory going. 9/11 was an 'inside insurance job'. Gun-control-obsessed 'libtards' had orchestrated every high school shooting in the US since 26 July 1764 – she was that specific. Covid-19 was a biological weapon designed by the Chinese and deployed against the West to 'take our civilisation down'. Though unpersuaded, I was impressed by her eloquent explanations and her knack for citing sources within academia, the military and the scientific and intelligence communities. Of course, I had no way of verifying them while sitting here with her sipping my Blanton's, but there was something alluring about *how* she communicated – quietly, politely, patiently – if not *what* she communicated. She was never hostile. She listened when it was her turn and didn't interject. Arlene would, at junctures, sportingly ask what I made of her arguments. 'Now how about that, Tooooom?'

Arlene's style warded off what could have been an anxious episode – the pulse revving and the face rubifying as I scrambled to think of witty comebacks and salvage data from the dusty cellars of my memory. We've all been there, as many arguments unfold like that. Not this one, though. I look back on it as an object lesson in the art of disagreement that might bring your adversary closer to your view – or has more chance than insulting and patronising them.

If my comrades at the Guildhall could take the Arlene approach and sit down with the fash, they might not change their minds – if Žižek is correct – but they might, through the calm application of empathy, start to realise the error in, for instance, at once loathing Jews and loving the Jewish homeland. This may not be such a challenge if another philosopher – more dulcet-toned than Žižek – called Peter Rollins is right. He claims that belief and unbelief are not so different states. The religious fundamentalist is never certain that God will look after *everything* otherwise why does he call an ambulance when his child gets sick or lock the doors of his church at night? These convictions are shaky because the real drivers of his fundamentalism are less to do with theology and more to do with unresolved despair and anxiety. Trying to refute this man's religious principles won't win him over, especially if whoever's doing the refuting is themselves displacing their angst onto another tenuous ideology. Better to create a space, Rollins says, that allows people on either side of a dispute 'to encounter our brokenness and our unknowing' so that 'we're not afraid of the other, not projecting onto the other'. It follows, then, that when people start to find inner peace in this way they are keener to reach an outer ceasefire with atheists or Muslims or the woke brigade or whichever other whipping boy or fall guy.

7

I hope that escaping the obscene site of stress that is Murtala Muhammed Airport will give me a break. Fat chance. As soon as Oge's older brother picks us up, he tells us that he narrowly avoided being mugged this morning as he stopped at traffic lights in the smart Ikeja district of Lagos, about five blocks from where we're driving now. His assailants pulled knives and he stamped his foot on the gas. Not helping matters, Oge recalls an aunt who wasn't so fortunate – her gold necklace was snatched from her throat while she was stuck in a gridlock. Her mistake was winding down her windows due to faulty air con.

We edge our way past low-rise apartment blocks painted in luminous colours and tin-roofed huts pitching beauty and nail treatments, 'men's wears', 'ladies' wears', shawarmas, Indomie noodles, soups and stews.

I try to lose myself in mobile solitaire while Oge and her brother riff on other fear-inducing topics. Oge complains about having paid over 340,000 naira (about £180) for Covid tests both on departure and arrival.

'Are they okay?' says her brother. 'We only had 3,000 deaths from it, whereas you had more than 200,000 in the UK.'

Oge kisses her teeth. 'Imagine! Nigeria just wants to be like other countries with the same regulations. Sheer nonsense.' She relates the hassle we copped flying here, Covid the oft-reached-for excuse. Our Royal Air Maroc plane was delayed leaving Heathrow by three hours, a frazzled agent informing us that 'extra Covid checks' were needed. A rotund British retiree with Yoruba family told of a huge backlog of Nigerians wanting to visit home after the lockdown. A guy in a Morocco football team shirt, who'd been to Qatar to watch his side's excellent run in the World Cup, thought that Covid had exacerbated what Royal Air Maroc have always done: greedily overbook seats. Our connecting flight in Tangiers bore the theory out – yet another hour's delay while passengers had to check their hand luggage into the hold.

Oge's brother, a well-connected businessman who owns a shopping centre, brings up the issue of what we might call 'non-travel anxiety'. In twenty years, he hasn't secured a visa to visit Britain. 'When they reject me,' he tuts, 'they say that I cannot prove where my money comes from. So now I have given up applying.' This is galling for someone who's sponsored six of his siblings to make new lives in the UK.

At our hotel there are more forms to fill out including an 'I definitely don't have Covid' disclaimer. How many have answered that honestly? In the lift to our room is a sign advising guests what to do in a 'civil unrest emergency'. 'Beware of strange bullets' catches my eye. It's a typo, presumably, but I try to visualise a 'strange bullet'. Does it have a surreal shape like a Picasso painting? Is a 'strange bullet' more painful than a stray one?

I awake to find Oge looking at Facebook on her phone. She's beaming at a video of a white woman in full Igbo finery speaking Nigerian pidgin English. Occasionally she switches out of this accent and into her native one, Estuary English. ''Ow am I doin', babe, yeah?'

If I was concerned about the cultural appropriation risks around being a fat white man soon to be pictured on social media in similar garb undergoing a traditional Igbo wedding, this surely takes the cake. I've already anticipated the headlines – or rather troll-posts: 'White Lecturer in Racist Dad-Dancing Scandal'. Remember the offence generated by Kim Kardashian wearing Fulani cornrows in her hair? Or Selena Gomez in a bindi and Indian-style dress? Or, zanily, a Chinese model for Dolce & Gabbana attempting to eat pizza and pasta with chopsticks?

'Isn't that sort of ... dodgy?' I ask Oge.

'Lord no, we respect her for integrating into our community. She has married an Igbo prince, learned our customs and our language, and is writing a book about it.'

I notice hundreds of warm comments and thumbs-up emojis under her post. 'Where's she from originally?'

'Hastings. Now she lives in Anambra province.'

'Extraordinary.' I can't help but giggle.

Oge scowls. 'Why do you make jest of her?'

'I'm just surprised that ...' I trail off. I'm not diplomatic enough to bridge the attitudinal gulf between us.

I lie back on the bed, flip between thoughts. Appropriation has always gone on between cultures. Shouldn't we save our indignation for racism that objectively harms people in genocides, wars, police brutality, prison-industrial complexes? On the other hand, this girl is sailing dangerously close to old-school minstrel shows or white thespians browning up to play Othello. But even nowadays there are contradictions to cancellation. Gentile actors still portray Jewish characters, sometimes hackneyed ones like the Faginesque Alfie Solomons in *Peaky Blinders*. Good actor he may be, Tom Hardy isn't Jewish.

8

For breakfast we're served another bureaucratic headache. The hotel's records show that only one prandium is attached to our double room.

'*Chai*!' Oge yawps at the desk clerk. I've been taught that '*chai*' doesn't directly translate into English but is an exclamation along the lines of 'oh my God!' or, in some contexts, 'damn'. 'There are two of us and so there must be two breakfasts!' she yawps.

'No, sister, will you look at the booking!' the clerk yawps back.

They yawp at each other some more, which does my nerves no good. They'd be in worse shape if I'd been thick enough to join the yawping myself. For very good postcolonial reasons, Nigerians have had enough of being yawped at by Westerners. I should have remembered that before yawping at Mr Epaulettes yesterday.

As Oge and the waiter keep yawping at each other and step near enough that they're virtually kissing, I must remind myself that in West Africa what can seem to the outsider like a furious quarrel is often normal discourse. Seldom are ill feelings meant. I learned this while working in Côte d'Ivoire a decade ago, when two guys in the street would seem to be on the brink of a punch-up before combusting into laughter and hugging. But it's jarring to see this kind of thing again, as most of the travelling I've done since Côte d'Ivoire has been in Southeast Asia, where raising your voice in public is as socially unacceptable as not paying for a round of drinks is in the UK.

As predicted, Oge and the waiter are now smiling as though nothing has happened. We sit down to boiled yams and egg sauce. Christmas decorations are up and the stereo plays the same three festive songs on a loop: the tolerable 'Feliz Navidad'; the execrable 'Wonderful Christmastime' by Paul McCartney; and the rather better 'Peace on Earth/Little Drummer Boy' performed by David Bowie and Bing Crosby. Having missed two meals yesterday, we finish our first course and return to the buffet. In addition to African cuisine there's a European-style spread of pastries and cold cuts. Oge forks salami onto her plate.

'That's pork, dear.'

'It is not.'

'Pretty sure it is.' I ask the waiter when he comes round, who confirms that it is indeed salami.

'See – it is salami,' says Oge.

'Which is pork.'

'But I ate something like this when I first moved to England, in Oxford. It was called ham.'

'That's pork too. It comes from a pig.'

'No, it is ham. It is called ham, so it is ham.'

I rub my forehead. 'As long as God doesn't strike you down for it, or whatever.'

Not wanting to lose face, Oge surreptitiously pushes the salami to the side of her plate.

'Incidentally, what *is* the pork ban all about? Why not prawns as well, if you're going to be kosher?'

'I can see that you are in a much better mood now, *abi*.'

'How so?'

'Because you are asking questions again. You are curious once more.' Oge puts her fork down. 'You should talk to my brother about the whole Hebrew-Igbo thing.'

Oge's brother calls to confirm the tour he'll give us today. It's kind of him and I'm intrigued by the schedule, which includes a visit to the late musician and political martyr Fela Kuti's shrine and dinner at a Chinese restaurant (dubbed 'continental food' in Nigerian English). At the same time, I'm anxious, you will be unsurprised to hear.

9

If travel anxiety can stem from being disorganised then it can also be provoked by being *too* organised. If spontaneity can bring unexpected mishaps, then erasing all spontaneity can be as calamitous as Charlie Sheen's downfall. I once was chatting to a retired man in a London pub who had, in his own words, 'done everywhere'. He went on to offer generic descriptions of the Colosseum, the Eiffel Tower, the Taj Mahal and other lionised sites that could have been read out from Tripadvisor. He didn't say if he enjoyed these places or found them interesting – he'd simply 'done' them, mentioning each as if working down a checklist. When I asked about his other memories of these destinations, he said that he'd 'done' carbonara in Rome and butter chicken in Agra. Again, he didn't express an opinion on these activities.

Things became clearer when the old boy said he'd travelled the world exclusively on guided tours. Even when given 'free periods' to explore on his own – like a prisoner allowed out for exercise once a day – he'd stayed in the hotel bar or popped to the nearest tourist-baiting restaurant or gift shop, but only one recommended by the operator. As someone for whom boredom and anxiety sometimes intersect, it was a struggle to listen to this old boy talking about what struck me as a regimented and soul-erasing way to see the world.

When my brother-in-law picks us up in his chauffeured 4x4, I stare out the window at the stream of faces, bodies, outfits, vehicles, businesses and buildings. I can't focus on any of it. The philosopher Alain de Botton has diagnosed a strain of dread that can infect travellers when they arrive at a destination and 'feel obliged to admire a sequence of things which have no connection to one another besides a geographic one and a proper understanding of which would require a range of qualities unlikely to be found in any one person'. This is true of all travellers at one time or another – it applies to me and perhaps to the old boy in that pub. Were his summaries of Paris or Rome or Agra down to a fear that he didn't understand the 'sequence of things' shown to him on those trips and so had no right to an opinion on them? The alienation that de Botton mentions could be worsened by the very format of the guided tour. Since he was just one of a herd of other tourists all being told the same thing and taken to the same places, perhaps the old boy was embarrassed because he suspected that others on that trip comprehended and appreciated things that he didn't. But if de Botton is right, the irony would be that all the old boy's tourmates might have suspected the same of him and each other.

The commercial nature of the guided tour must play a part in this malaise. Corners are cut in an industry where time is money and your host is maxing profit by underpaying your drivers and guides, and block-booking you and others into hotels and eateries. While there are good and bad organised tours, of course, the latter prizes speed over reflection and quantity over quality of experience. We shouldn't be shocked, then, if punters come away from such dismal gigs only able to trade in clichés and truisms.

Near the end of our pints, the old boy let slip what he truly, personally thought about at least one thing he'd 'done' travel-wise: 'I was disappointed with the pyramids in Egypt. We drove by pretty fast in a bus and the driver pointed out the window and said, "There you are." Two minutes later, the pyramids were gone.'

Having a timetable of things to do in Lagos is making me feel *obliged* to enjoy them. Just as de Botton confesses to having (on one trip to Madrid) preferred to stay in bed and wait for his flight home rather than go out and sight-see, I'm now racking my brains for an excuse to head back to our hotel and do precisely nothing for the rest of the day. Part of this angst of anticipation is down to my crossed purposes here in Nigeria. On the one hand, this is supposed to be a holiday – it's happening over the Christmas break and I'm on leave from my job. At the same time, I'm getting married, which makes this different to a lazy vacation. Duty and pressure are involved. My new in-laws' eyes are on me, sizing me up as a worthy husband. On top of all this, I'm a writer who's never really 'off duty' wherever he goes. I'll always be noting images, ideas, encounters.

10

What am I doing here? We've all asked ourselves this. Like the terror of death, the terror of not knowing what you're doing in life, not knowing what your purpose is, goes to the nub of why we get anxious. There could be something fundamentally human about it, since we're the only animals to question our own existence. The terror might stem from the expectations society has of us, which takes us back to the Lacanian symbolic. There's a set of public expectations – or clichés? – about what an academic should be: studious; curious; independent-spirited and so on. And those corresponding to a journalist: tenacious; brave; fair-minded. There are norms defining a modern man, what he should be, his responsibilities. Same for a husband. Though I'm not feeling the burn of reaching for these ideals consciously, I might be unconsciously. It's a tall order since nobody can ever achieve these ideals – that's why they're called ideals, dictionary definition: 'existing only in the imagination; desirable or perfect but not likely to become a reality'.

In an unusual travel situation like this – one doesn't get married in rural Nigeria every day – sensitivities about my identity are heightened. Aside from not knowing if I should be behaving as an academic, a travel writer, a tourist, a husband-to-be or all of the above, I may be unconsciously freaking out about whether I can perform any of these roles. Can I ever be that excellent academic? That excellent husband? That almost no one reaches these dizzy heights doesn't change the symbolic order's dictates to us. The most eloquent reflection I've read on the push-me, pull-you stresses of identity is Tobias Wolff's mind-blowing memoir *This Boy's Life*. In it, a pre-teen desperado who frequently ups sticks and relocates somewhere new on his mother's whim, is torn between the two magnetic forces of 1950s America: the gun and the Bible. He spends afternoons in his apartment aiming his rifle at passers-by through the window, revelling in the 'ecstasy of my power over them'. One day, he can't help but pull the trigger on a squirrel and, this being the US of A, nobody notices, apart from the squirrel, of course. His hankering to become a macho 'real Westerner' deserts him. He locates the squirrel's carcase, buries it under a cross made from ice lolly sticks and cries himself to sleep. A couple of weeks later, he tries out the routine again – this time without pulling the trigger – and is consumed by panic when he sees his catechism instructor Sister James coming up the steps to the front door. 'What would she think? What would she make of the rifle, the fur hat, the uniform, the darkened room? What would she make of me? I feared her disapproval but even more than that, even her amusement, at what she could not possibly understand. I didn't understand it myself.'

The issue of what I should be and do is further muddied by capitalist society's yardsticks for success. I hate to be cynical, but arse-licking, crowd-pleasing and rat-racing are more likely to take you to the top of most industries than anything else. In the increasingly mercenary academe, a shortcut to making professor is to solicit research cash from arms dealers and pollution-spouters. Equally, I could have sold out years ago and got a plum job on a tabloid rag by writing transphobic and migrant-slamming fake news. But some of us have weird hang-ups about… what are the words I'm looking for? Ethics, integrity, that sort of stuff. One thing I learned from selling out at the start of my career was not to bloody well do it again.

11

We're snared in slow-moving traffic on the Eko Bridge that links Lagos Island to the mainland. I'm staring out the dirt-smeared window at the lagoon. A hench fisherman leans over the side of a sickle-shaped rowing boat and drags a net stuffed with writhing opaline fish. He struggles with it like a powerlifter in an Olympic final. His colleague, perched tenuously close to the edge of the stern, stamps his oar on the hull of the boat and titters at his mate's duel with nature. With a last heave, the fisherman drops the net full of *shawa* herring into the boat and gives his colleague a high five. At the risk of sounding like the Western chump romanticising native life, the work seems rewarding. These guys are clearly enjoying themselves, they're socialising, they're outside, they're moving their bodies. These are advantages over other jobs, North or South. They can't be well-paid or have much hope for promotion. They must see better-off people all the time driving along this bridge and in movies and in memes and on billboards.

'Do you think those fishermen worry about their status in life?' I ask Oge.

She laughs wickedly, but also alluringly. 'Imagine! Why would they? They are doing what they have to do.'

We're interrupted by a young girl in flip-flops and pyjamas who presses a supersized packet of plantain chips against the car window. She releases one hand to make a tiny fist and bang on the window. I shake my head. She bangs again. I shake my head again. It takes three more shakes to persuade her to move on to the *keke* autorickshaw behind us.

'You know that almost 80 per cent of Nigerians work in the informal sector?' Oge says. While I wouldn't always trust a trained economist, I'll make an exception for her, although I'm biased.

'What kinds of jobs?'

'What that girl is doing. What those boys in the boat are doing. Also, market traders, unlicensed shopkeepers, construction workers, maids, nannies. They might pay taxes, they might not. They will not have insurance or other protections. It is very different to Europe.'

I'm not sure if it is these days. Whatever hurdles I faced as a youth finding a job and making a life, the young people I teach are facing a much harsher world of precarious work – if they can find work – weaker unions, mounting student debt, decaying public services, exorbitant rents and zilcho chance of getting on the housing ladder. In 2011, Arianna Huffington published *Third World America*, a book whose title cunningly reflected its thesis ... that America was turning into the Third World. The UK must be there too and you don't have to be a social psychologist to know that the mental health effects ain't pretty.

But it helps if you *are* a social psychologist. Some of them wrote a report for the Mental Health Foundation which proved that social and economic inequality feeds depression and anxiety like a crate of worms will fatten a piranha. Children in low-income households are twice as likely to be mentally unwell than those in better-off homes. Over a third of jobless people are debilitated by mental distress, a tricky hole to get out of since over half of potential bosses are reluctant to employ those with such a history. Place has an influence too, as 'a person's neighbourhood environment can also reinforce isolation and exclusion' and 'living in an urban environment is a known risk factor for depression and anxiety'. You'll be more vulnerable still if you're on the wrong side of the inequality line *and* you're female, LGBTQ+, BAME, refugee or asylum seeker, disabled, have learning difficulties, are lonely or older. This is not a brokenness that can be fixed with more mindfulness or therapy, as 'People from poorer economic circumstances are still more likely to have worse mental health, even if they have been supported to develop good emotional and cognitive skills.' Instead, a new political and economic settlement is needed, urge the authors of the report, in which work is purposeful, low-stress, fairly waged and employees are protected from adverse conditions. 'Building a society in which people are less worried about their financial circumstances and more economically equal has the potential to reduce stress and anxiety,' they conclude.

12

Oge's brother is admirably well-travelled. He's so laid back I doubt he's prone to anxiety on the road. But you never know. He's been to most other African countries, much of mainland

Europe, Pakistan, India, Nepal, China and the United States. He's never seen much of these places outside of hotel rooms and boardrooms.

'Ever had trouble in these destinations?' I ask him.

'In Karachi we drove through a riot. A lot of pepper bodies.'

'What's a pepper body?'

'You have heard me use the term before,' Oge interjects.

'I don't recall.'

'You weren't listening.'

'It means angry person,' says Oge's brother.

'Did you feel unsafe in the car?'

'A little. It was better to stay in it than to leave. Like all things, it came to an end.'

He explains what will happen at our traditional wedding next week in Anambra, Oge's and his home province in eastern Nigeria. I don't follow everything he says, as the protocol is complicated. Since I don't have any relatives or friends accompanying me, some locals will be selected to form 'my family'. They will join me in 'negotiation' for the 'bride price' and other formalities.

'I just remembered something!' exclaims Oge. 'There was a story in the press recently about a white man who was due to marry an Igbo – like you. He travelled to the village of his betrothed and started negotiating for the dowry. At first, the family asked for small amounts of money to buy yams and plantains. The man agreed. Then the relatives requested 1 million naira (about £100) to cover school fees for the children. He said yes to that, too. When they started talking about many millions of naira, the man got nervous and went to the toilet. He never came back!'

Oge and her brother convulse with laughter. I manage a polite guffaw.

When a waiter brings us a steaming bowl of noodle soup, Oge's brother checks there's no pork in it. This feels like the time to ask him about Igbo traditions.

'They say that we are derived from the Jews who went south instead of to the Middle East, after freeing themselves from the Egyptians. Not eating swine is one habit we have retained. There are others. When an Igbo dies abroad, their body has to be repatriated back to Igboland like Jews to Israel. During the Biafra war in the late sixties when the Nigerian government was backed by *you British* and the Russians, Israel supported us, as did Jews in the US. One of our heroes is Bruce Mayrock, who set himself on fire in New York to protest the war.'

'Like that monk in Vietnam?'

'Yes, but Mayrock was studying to be a rabbi. Did you know that President Nixon and his advisor Kissinger considered sending troops to come to our aid? If he had then two million plus Igbos might not have perished.'

That would have been about the only ethical foreign intervention those two ever managed, I think to myself. 'I take it you lost family in that war?'

'Yes. Genocide is the more correct term.'

'How did it start?'

'Igboland declared independence, but Nigeria would not accept it. They wanted to keep hold of our oil and sell it to the UK, the Soviet Union and other countries.'

'Is there still a yearning for independence now?'

'If you had a referendum now then 99 per cent of Igbos would vote to be free.'

13

Our next destination is the New Afrika Shrine in honour of Fela Kuti. It's mobbed by food hawkers and youths hanging out. As we reverse into a parking space, three of them wave us in, hoping for a tip. Realising they'll have to split the donation, they jostle each other for pole position as our only guide. Oge's brother points to his driver's rearview camera. 'This is more efficient than any human eye, but in Nigeria everyone is a hustler.'

We exit the car, he tosses coins to the hustlers. Oge holds my hand. This is like a red rag to another hustle. A man with crimson-dyed dreadlocks speaks Igbo to Oge and then gives me a high-five. 'You are my in-law, sir. You have Christmas present for me, sir?'

Beside the door to the shrine is a sign in blue font against an orange background: 'The secret of life is to have no fear'.

'Easier said than done,' I whisper.

'What was that?' asks Oge.

'Nothing, dear.'

At the core of the shrine is a music venue with stage, amps, speakers and a bar. No one's performing tonight and the crowd is small. Oge and her brother deter other schemers with discreet head shakes. We go upstairs to a mezzanine and into a library of Fela's socialist and anti-colonial books. It's one of several recreations of the original Afrika Shrine, which was burned down by soldiers in 1977. They didn't much like Fela's resistance to the military junta of the time. The junta made him a prisoner of conscience in 1984. I have faint childhood memories of Shakespearean actors demanding his release on TV on behalf of Amnesty International.

I've long admired Fela but I'm in no mood to spend longer here. I feel so foreign, so white, so square. I'm tired of being hassled. I'm relieved when Oge's brother suggests we call it a day.

He drops us at the hotel. By way of farewell he says, 'Tom – if you can survive Lagos, you can survive anywhere.'

Oge heads to bed while I opt for a nightcap. I sit outside on a lounger by the hotel pool. I'm chilled enough to absorb the moment, to savour my whisky and listen to the trickle of the fountain and the fizz of the subdued late-night traffic. I focus only on those things rather than projecting back or forth to worrisome events past or yet to come. Even the odd mosquito bite doesn't annoy me. I'm on anti-malaria meds. I'll put some cream on later. I can let this slide.

'Hey, man, you see the football?' asks a Westerner in an accent that I can't place. He's sitting with his trainer-clad feet up on a table and is the spitting image of the actor Christoph Waltz.

'Sorry, no.'

He lights a cigarette and glares at his phone through the smoke. 'I can't get online to see the result. Anyway, no one cares about F91 Dudelange.' He raises an eyebrow.

'Where are they from?'

'Luxembourg, like me. I am Luc.'

'You're not Christoph Waltz?'

'Who is he?'

'Never mind. I'm Tom. Do you live in Nigeria?'

'No, no. In Kenya. I'm working here on the national power grid.' He raises his eyebrow again, grinds out his cigarette and lights another immediately. 'I run an engineering company.

We get called out all over Africa. There is not enough scientific education in these countries, so power grids go wrong all the time.'

'Do you know Lagos very well?'

'No. I just go from this hotel to the office and back. Every day.'

'Anywhere you'd recommend going?'

Up goes the eyebrow again. 'Not really. Victoria Island is supposed to be good. They have nature there. Or something.'

'How does Nigeria compare to Kenya?' I shouldn't have asked, it'll give him another excuse to moan.

'Nigerians are too rough. Kenyans are gentler. I have been in Kenya fifteen years. I am married.' He pauses and stares at me. 'Are you married to a Nigerian?'

'I've come here to do just that.'

He picks up his cigarettes and stands. 'Good luck. See you around.'

Over my years of travelling anxiously I've depended too much on drinking myself to sleep. It doesn't work tonight. Though I've no doubt my troubles are of the spirit, my main physical annoyance is a racing heartbeat. I try meditating. As is typical of the battle to fall sleep, I doze off when I stop trying to.

14

'We need the mall,' Oge announces first thing next morning.

'Who *needs* a mall?' I yawn, hankering for more rest. Sleep deprivation doesn't help the bothered bonce.

As our taxi reverses out of the hotel car park, a security guard steps out and taps on the boot, which is only three quarters shut.

'Every day I fix this up,' protests the driver, 'and it break again.'

'Fix it proper next time,' orders the guard.

The driver kisses his teeth as we proceed. 'Everywhere I go, this bother me. I cannot afford the fix, O.' He looks over his shoulder to Oge. 'Aunty, I'm telling you, this is haunting me like ghost.'

Oge cackles and pats him on the shoulder. She says something in Igbo that seems to soothe him.

We're stopped again at a police roadblock. An officer with pupils fogged by cataracts opens my door.

'Welcome, sir. What are you doing in Nigeria, sir?'

'I'm getting married.'

'Where, sir?'

'In Anambra State.'

The officer laughs. 'Igboland!' He nods approvingly at Oge. 'So, you marry Igbo girl. Nice Igbo girl. I am Igbo, too. Will you pick me for your wedding?'

'Pardon?'

'Will you invite me to your wedding?'

'Er ...' I look to Oge, who shrugs. 'Sure, if you happen to be in the area.'

The officer places his nightstick on the seat next to me and holds out his hands. 'Will you give me cake? Will you give me palm wine?'

'I don't see why not if you make it along.'

'Maybe champagne?'

'That, too, if we have it.'

There's a devastatingly awkward pause. Did I say the wrong thing? Is he going to arrest me? Beat me up? The officer snatches up his night stick and bids us a curt farewell.

We drive on. Oge shakes her head. 'Did you not understand what that was about?'

I think I do now, belatedly. 'I was supposed to give him a bribe?'

'Of course.'

'Why didn't you say something, then?' My chest tautens, stomach slumps. 'You know I'm trying to … integrate here … as best I can,' I say in a whiny tone. Oge squeezes my hand. *I should have been more savvy, having lived and worked in the Global South.*

If people are incongruous, so are places. As we stutter along the Oshodi–Egba Road, there are as many billboards praising God as there are pledging to make you rich quick. One sign combines these sentiments, reading 'Heaven Economics: Financial Conquest'. If he made his comeback today, this might shock the Humble Servant who travelled by foot, lived in poverty and chased the money changers out of the Temple of Jerusalem. In Lagos the state is both conspicuously present and absent. Other signage gestures to ministries, customs offices, police stations, military posts. The only medical services I spot are private and elite. There are folks in myriad official uniforms standing on pavements playing with their phones, crossing the road, squatting on the roofs of jeeps and trucks. At the same time, the ubiquity of beggars, unlicensed vendors and private security goons, from geriatrics in green berets barely able to lift their antique carbines to double-hard bastards in jackboots and bulletproof vests, suggests that the state has retreated from many of its duties.

Colourless and cracked, the mall's façade is embossed with luminous red, white and purple brands: 'Genesis Cinema'; 'TN Max'; 'Larboni Cakes and Froghurt'. A pillar is plastered with prohibitions: 'No Pets'; 'No Firearms'; 'No Photography'; 'No Skating'; 'No Smoking'. I'm not a dad yet but I can't resist a dad joke: 'Looks like we'll have to cancel our afternoon of wild abandon, darling.'

We flop down in a rooftop restaurant overlooking what's nominally a car park but is more like a bustling square. Some vehicles are parked and others, including minivans with passengers standing on their rear bumpers, are coming and going at a furious rate. Women in headscarves kneel before sacks of soda bottles. Men push trolleys overflowing with car parts. Children squat on plywood tables under parasols next to coolboxes. Above them all is an extraordinary sight – blue-red mid-morning sunlight stippled by close-knit cirrocumulus clouds like bubble wrap. It could be a Fernando Amorsolo painting and we can't take our eyes off it.

As if the gods are conspiring against me, I receive an ominous text message. 'Dr T G Sykes, please contact T— Medical Practice urgently.' Brilliant. Just bloody brilliant. A fortnight before flying to Nigeria, I underwent the yearly tests recommended for middle-aged men – especially those who don't look after themselves. They took some 'bloods' and gave me a chest X-ray. The day before I left, I called the surgery and an admin said that all the results were fine. Now this. Now I'm imagining some gruesome lump on my lungs or bold typeface on a spreadsheet declaring '**LEUKAEMIA**'.

'Any chance of wifi here?' I ask. 'I could try and send them a WhatsApp message.'

'None at all,' says Oge. 'It will be fine. We will have lunch and then phone from the hotel.'

She's right, of course. I should let this lie, since uncertainty is a fact of the traveller's life. Many things don't go to plan. You never know what to expect from a destination, especially if it's new to you. The usual comforts and privileges of home can be in short supply when you're abroad. All of which should be part of travel's thrill and often has been for me. And it would be now if I wasn't already at a baseline of anxiety due to other factors that I'm trying to figure out.

'Sod it, I'll make an international call and go to debtors' prison.' I dial the number with the UK code and get a beeping noise. I try it again and a Nigerian woman's voice informs me, 'The number you have dialled is not recognised.'

'Well, it should be – I typed it in right!' I shout at her. She doesn't respond. It's a recorded message. I stand up, hyperventilating. 'We need to go, dear. Now.'

Now no taxis are going directly from the mall, so we must catch a *keke*. It's a bumpy ride, a literal pain in the arse. All the way I can't rid my head of the worst-case scenario – collapsing from a stroke and dying in a gridlocked ambulance before I reach a hospital.

I dash inside our hotel room and call the practice again. Same annoying voice message. I WhatsApp my dad and ask him to call them on my behalf. He rings me back five minutes later and says there's nothing to worry about, just that I'm inching towards pre-diabetic. That's not enough to reassure me – nothing ever is for the anxious traveller – especially as too much food and drink was going to be my crutch for the next two weeks.

'You know that the animists here design their own gods to look after them,' says Oge.

'Are there any anti-anxiety gods?' I reply. 'I could carry an effigy of one around my neck.'

15

I'm liking Chinua Achebe Airport before I arrive there, for it's named after a fine writer. That's good kismet. It surely has an advantage over airports I've been to that were named after people who fell foul of the aviation industry in some way. NAIA Airport in Manila alludes to a politician, Benigno 'Ninoy' Aquino, who was shot dead by political enemies as he stepped off a plane ... in that very same airport when it was called Manila International Airport, abbreviated to MIA. When I think of MIA, I think of 'Missing in Action', which could also be tempting fate in an air travel context. In India in 2007, I flew out of Dum Dum Airport, now Netaji Subhas Chandra Bose International Airport, in honour of a politician who died in a plane crash in Taiwan in 1945. While I haven't visited myself, Lima's Jorge Chávez International Airport commemorates a renowned aviator who perished in 1910 when his fragile Blériot XI went down in the Pennine Alps. You'd think that even nations with small populations could find at least one hero who hadn't expired in a plane wreck to immortalise with an airport appellation. Although John F. Kennedy, John Lennon, Indira Gandhi or Yitzhak Rabin didn't die on or near a plane, calling an airport after someone who was assassinated might also be inviting Nemesis.

Anyway, outside Chinua Achebe Airport is a radically different landscape to Lagos. It feels like a radically different country, too – why Oge's people fought for their independence, I guess. It's much drier, the dust-swept main road belted by taupe bluffs interspersed with cadaverous palm trees. Further out, a cryptic haze hangs over the bush. On our drive there's a petrol station every half mile. Outside one, a yellow-jumpsuited attendant is dancing along a line of vehicles.

'Oil,' says Oge. 'This is why the Yorubas fought us. But oil is dear now. It's cheaper in the morning, so people will park overnight to get a good place in the queue.'

In Oge's village we overtake a teenage mum and her baby daughter on a scooter. We pass two young men whipping each other with long canes. An indigenous sport, Oge assures me. The family home is a white mansion. A man in glasses and a prayer cap opens the iron gates to let us in. I put my hand on my heart and bid him, '*Salaam alaikum*.' The man recoils with surprise and says, '*Wa alaikum salam*.'

'What did you say to him?' asks Oge, as we unpack the car.

'A greeting you give to Muslims.'

'My family has employed Mohammed for twenty years and I never thought about him being Muslim.'

We're mobbed by assorted kids – my new nieces, nephews, younger cousins. It takes a good half hour to greet them all plus parents – my new cousins and siblings-in-law. Oge distributes presents, mostly Western branded clothing.

I sit on the porch with her parents. I'm now to call them 'Mum' and 'Dad' as if they were my own. Rather sweet, I think.

It works both ways, according to the novel I am reading. *Purple Hibiscus*, set in Igboland in the 1980s, mentions an animist belief that when a man marries a woman, his whole family marries her too. Incidentally, the author of the book, Chimamanda Ngozi Adichie, is currently visiting her home village near here, where she'll be receiving the title of honorary chief.

Physically, Mum and Dad couldn't be more dissimilar. Dad is short and wiry, like a long-distance runner, while Mum is tall and well-built.

'You can see that my siblings and I took after Mum,' laughs Oge, 'and not Dad, who is like a little boy at age 79.' Dad's hearing isn't great – probably just as well.

Dad discusses wedding plans. He confirms that the village has nominated in-laws to represent me, as this is key to the ceremony. 'Why did your own family not come?'

'Mostly my relatives couldn't afford it or take the time away from work to attend.' I elect not to mention that my mum – who has been to India, Mexico and other demanding destinations – decided almost last-minute not to come due to concerns about the heat, the traffic, the security situation and the fact that she's not far off 70.

He pinches his nose and studies the tiles under our feet. I try to guess what he's thinking, imbuing him with my fears about privilege, about abysses between sets of values. *White people can't afford to come to Nigeria? Are they frightened they'll get sick from our spicy food or sunburned or robbed? Don't they care about their own family member on the most important day of his life?*

Instead, Dad says, 'That is a shame.' He says that my pseudo-relatives will help me with the bride price negotiations.

The negotiations are symbolic – I'm not actually buying my wife. It doesn't work like that these days, just as it hasn't in Europe since the Middle Ages. Whether it's the beer, the creeping anxiety, the heat or a combo of the three, I don't follow the rest of his instructions. I guess I'll find out on the day. What I'm most afraid of is having to dance because I'll look like a total numpty.

'Does the ceremony have anything to do with juju?' I ask Dad.

He crosses himself. 'I am a believer in the Lord Jesus Christ.'

'I wanted to know if the traditional religion here, before Christianity–'

Dad's head wobbles like a flimsy pan at boiling point. He gestures to Oge. She comes over and he continues speaking to me in Igbo, her translating.

'You do not play with juju. Twenty years ago, a young woman moved into our village, married a resident and had a daughter with him. The couple separated soon after. The woman relocated to her village of origin, leaving her daughter behind with her husband's family. This is unusual in our culture. When she grew to be a teenager, the daughter travelled to visit her mother and never returned. Rumour had it that the daughter was forced to remain in her mother's village.

'Years later, a man from that village came to us and demanded land. He said it was the daughter's birth right and that he had come to claim it on her behalf. It is hard to know here which land belongs to whom, so he appropriated some plots by having men build fences around them. When my nephew questioned these men, they beat him badly.

'The man from the other village calls himself a juju man. He says he has cast spells to protect his plots. Trespassers will die. His house is full of objects invested with bad juju: amulets; the roots of certain plants and trees; the skulls of monkeys and snakes. If you go near these you will get sick. The juju man has told us that he has written my name and the names of the other village elders onto pieces of paper. He has placed them inside boxes with locks requiring several keys. This way he can control our destinies – if we cross him he will rain misfortune on us. The juju man is selling this stolen land on for a lot of money. But nobody dares to oppose him.'

I ask Oge why Dad's scared to stand up to this charlatan when he has Jesus on his side.

'People here believe in a mix of things. The old ways die hard.'

'Surely this guy can't *actually* control anything with these plants and bits of paper?'

'It does not matter. What matters is that people believe that he can. They are scared – that is the most powerful belief.'

Dad breaks off to berate the kids for throwing stones at a chicken. 'Hey, that is our dinner!' Sure enough, our uber-fresh chicken stew is served an hour later. It's disturbing how different – and how much better – it tastes than meat from a British supermarket that's been pumped full of chemicals and sent round the world twice. I feel like someone who previously had no sense of smell suddenly being able to enjoy the aromas of jasmine and honeysuckle. Even pleasanter, we absorb this ambrosia as the sun goes down and the temperature cools and the tree frogs trill and the cicadas … make whatever noise cicadas make. I learned to adore West African evenings in Côte d'Ivoire in the 2010s.

We leave the family home at 8pm. We're enveloped by a sandstorm.

'It's not a sandstorm,' Oge fact-checks.

Okay, it's not a sandstorm, it's a shed load of dust whipped up by 'useless' – Oge's word, not mine – motorists who've chosen to drive on the more churned-up side of the dirt track. The road less gravelled, as it were. Normally everyone takes the firmer lane, only tonight 'people are in a rush – it is holiday time', Oge says. And the upshot of this speed-freakery is that we can't see three inches through the peppery pall. Combined with the darkness, it's a formidable barrier to progress, supposing we don't want a car crash. I fret about road safety in Nigeria. I know too much about it from masochistic web browsing. Almost 12,000 people died in car wrecks here last year and Nigeria ranks in the top several most hazardous nations in terms of fatalities. There's little enforcement of sobriety or seatbelt-wearing. Drivers are almost never prosecuted when they run someone over.

'C-can we pull over?' I squeak. 'Wait for the storm to pass?'

Oge scoffs. '*Chai!* And wait for kingdom come?'

I scrunch my eyes up, clamp my teeth together and send another prayer to nowhere – *please don't let us get mangled in a pile-up!*

16

We're staying in a sparkling and spacious apartment inside a gargantuan hotel equipped with a gym and a pool area that morphs into an entertainment venue after dark. But it's another grim night for me with my heart walloping away. Oge falls asleep well before me and I feel terribly alone. I finally sleep after several podcast episodes. The experts say that such stimulae only keeps you awake but I have to take my mind off the speeding ticker somehow.

When I come around, Oge has already showered and dressed. She's putting her make-up on at the dresser by our bed. Though my heart rate has normalised I'm still nauseous. I start crying and this takes me by surprise – I didn't will it. Is this my unconscious looking out for me, trying to ascertain whether the woman I'm about to spend the rest of my life with will be sympathetic to my plight, my disability even?

Oge runs her fingers through my hair. 'What is wrong, sweetie?'

'I've been really battling with anxiety since we got to Nigeria.'

'Are you having second thoughts about marrying me? I would rather you told me now.'

'No, absolutely not. I love you and I'm looking forward to the wedding.' From what I know about how the psyche works I may not mean what I just said. I may not know that I don't mean what I just said.

'It is strange,' says Oge. 'Since I have known you, I have seen you as a confident person. You have travelled to Africa before, you have dealt with situations more stressful than this one.'

'I know. My anxiety is a conundrum. I can't predict when it will strike.'

Fortunately, today is a free day with no obligations to travel or socialise. After breakfast we go to the gym. Half an hour on the treadmill releases endorphins and other happy chemicals. I should do this every day. I probably won't, though.

We head outside to the swimming pool. Egged on by Oge's sister-in-law cracking open a Guinness (in Nigeria it's just called a stout) at 11am, I get on the Heineken myself. I swim, sunbathe and read a colleague's journal paper that I promised to give feedback on before the holiday ends. Oge, her sister and sister-in-law vanish for a while to talk wedding business and I'm left in charge of four hyperactive kids. The youngest, Ebube, isn't so confident in the water. I hold her while she flaps her arms and legs in an approximation of swimming.

I lift her out of the pool when she's tired. She points to the skin graft on my calf. 'How did you do that, Uncle Tom?' she asks.

'I was born with it.'

'Like you are born with your hair?'

'Yes.'

'I was born with hair but I wasn't born with *that*.'

'Not everyone is born with *this*.'

'Did you scratch it?'

'No, but it …' I trail off. No need to inflict a four-year-old with my gory medical history.

Children can be astonishingly discreet, which is maybe why she asks me, 'Did a doctor make it better?'

'Yes, exactly that.' I slap on a fresh layer of sun cream.

'Why are you putting that on?' asks Ebube.

'Because my skin will burn if I don't.'

'Can *I* put it on?'

'Not sure. We'll ask your mum when she's back.'

We're cut off by a brawl between the other kids – all boys, of course. It's comical as the belligerents aren't able enough swimmers to reach each other, their anger stifled by having to focus on keeping their heads above the water. When one gets within a few feet of another, he tries to throw a punch but it's blocked and slowed by the water. That's lucky, as I wouldn't want to have to explain to their mum how a black eye or bruised cheek materialised on my watch. Instead, there's a lot of thrashing around with water flying in eyes. Whining and weeping follow.

'Stop that!' I call out. 'Let's all come in now and have a rest.'

The boys freeze, droop their heads in shame. Miserably, they make their way to the pool ladder.

I turn to Ebube. She's managed to empty the entire tube of sun cream over her head. I snatch the tube from her and start wiping the gunk off her with a tissue. She flinches as I do it, expecting a reprimand. 'Don't worry,' I say, 'tricky to get the hang of these things.'

The women return with Cokes for the kids. Won't the sugar and caffeine only make them more hyper?

Just before sunset Oge receives a phone call. I only hear her side of the conversation and it's ill-boding. '10,000?' she exclaims. 'What about the invoice, brother?' She speaks in Igbo for a while, sounding ever more frantic.

Oh shite, I think, *is something going wrong with the wedding? An unpaid bill? An unavailable service? Will there be no food or – worse, from my perspective – no drink?*

Oge puts on a tinny, child-like voice and says in English, 'Please, sir. I am in the hospital and I need my food and my medications. Please, sir.'

I frown at her.

She ignores me, keeps talking on the phone. 'Please have mercy for us, sir. God will bless you.' She ends the call and cackles.

'What the fuck was that about?' I gasp. Lying beside us on sunloungers, sister and sister-in-law remove their sunglasses in shock. 'Sorry about the language.'

Oge does a celebratory dab. 'It was an acting job. I deserve an Oscar!'

She tells me that our driver, Emmanuel, has been stopped by police for speeding. 'It is a cook-up,' she says, as they wanted to fine him without giving him a receipt. In other words, a bribe. Oge pretended to be a sick relative needing an urgent visit. It worked, as the police forgave Emmanuel and let him go on his way – in truth to a football match.

17

'You are shaking,' says Oge. We drive past a billboard with a photo of a handsome dude in a red velvet *isi agu* top. A caption below him reads, '46 years old. Painful exit.' I assume this is about his death, but I also take it as a bad omen for me.

I look down to my own outfit. It's not as natty as his but it's traditional Igbo. I feel ridiculously self-conscious. I've never had any sartorial sense and, since I started putting on weight in my early thirties, clothes – Western or otherwise – haven't looked good on me. But most of all I'm worried about the old cultural appropriation chestnut. Photos of me making an absolute knob of myself in this gear, trying to dance and trying not to look terrified, will soon be doing the rounds on social media.

The courtyard of the family home has been transformed. Two marquees are up, long dining tables and a DJ booth beneath them. A battalion of friends and relatives are chopping veg, pounding yams, plucking chickens, roasting goats and stirring church-bell-sized cauldrons of stew. The aroma all about us is a cross of barbecuing meat, spiky spices and minty petrichor.

Oge climbs out of the car, holding up her great flowing dress to avoid the dirt on the ground. She points to two tethered goats. 'It is traditional for the happy couple to take these away with them after the ceremony. I think we will struggle to get them on the plane, O.'

We're led upstairs to a photographer who forces us into multiple poses. Hold hands. Face her. Put your hands on her shoulders. Lean forward. Lean backward. Move this way a little. Move that way a little. I hate being photographed at the best of times. I hate having to smile when I don't feel like smiling. I know these pictures are going to come out with me looking profoundly uncomfortable.

Oge disappears with her sisters and other females. I'm led into the kitchen where my makeshift relatives are sitting at a table with my authentic new in-laws. Everyone here is male. There's an extensive debate between my pseudo-relatives and Oge's dad and his relatives. It's in Igbo and I don't understand a word. I try to decode the body language. There's as much smiling as there are pensive frowns and pauses. I still don't understand anything. At least I'm allowed a beer while this goes on – it doesn't last long.

One of my pseudo-relatives rises from his chair. He beckons me to follow him and two others into the toilet. Once we've all squeezed in there, trying not to step in the pissoir, he asks, 'Do you have money?'

I gracelessly pull out a wad of naira from my pocket. The pseudo-relative plucks a few notes out. We return to the kitchen and there's another half hour of discussion. We go back to the toilet. 'Let us offer a little more for the bride price,' proposes my pseudo-relative.

'Take what you want.'

More negotiation. Finally, Dad accepts the offer. A round of handshakes. I start for the door, thinking we're done here, only Dad slips me back the money I just gave him and speaks more Igbo.

Fuck! I roar inwardly. *Have I just been rejected? Has Dad decided I'm not good enough for his darling daughter? I'm some fat, decadent Westerner who belongs to the same bunch of bastards who ran his country for sixty years – and he'd be old enough to remember the final twenty?*

My pseudo-relative translates. 'Father says you are an honest man, so there is no need to pay the bride price. Father is certain that you will look after his daughter. Instead, you are invited to give something to Mother for the effort she has made to arrange this wedding.'

Mum saunters into the kitchen, accepts my dosh and bows her head to me. I bow, too. Seems only fair.

We go out to the marquee where the guests are taking their seats. There is no set mealtime, with folks eating as and when they arrive. Thus, younger relatives are constantly ferrying ice buckets of beer, wine and palm wine and trays of 'small chops': spring rolls; chicken gizzards; puff-puff (sort of dough balls) and other snacks. I sit down at a table with my pseudo-relatives opposite Oge's parents and elders. I have no appetite so I keep boozing. I'm going to have to dance later and possibly do some public speaking. I need liquid bravery.

The DJ strikes up with bombastic Afrobeat. The poles of the marquee shake. It's just as well none of my pseudo-relatives chat to me as I wouldn't be able to hear them. Soon enough, Oge and her women relatives, all stunning in their matching green dresses and headgear, dance into the space between her folks and my pseudo-relatives and me. Oge looks at me desirously as she shakes her hips and shuffles her shoulders and bends her knees and claps her hands. She and her girls soon dance off out of sight. Ten minutes later they repeat the procedure. Oge told me this morning that it's a custom whereby a fiancée has to woo her betrothed with moves busted well enough to convince him that he's made the right choice in marrying her. This is all very well but in my anxious state I wish we could skip to the getting married part.

The dance-on, dance-off manoeuvre happens for a third time. And then there's a wait, a long, long wait. I drink more palm wine and beer. I feel sufficiently lubricated to at least nibble on some *chin chin* (crispy fried dough). If I were in a better mental place I'd find this delicious. Instead, it tastes like nails. I need to get it into my stomach so that I don't pass out at some key moment in the proceedings. That's a big ask. I have to wash the single mouthful I can tolerate down with a third of a bottle of Heineken.

I wait some more. I drink a lot more. I wait a lot more. Time is really dragging now. The music reduces in volume – is this a signal something's about to happen? Nope. Eventually, I pluck up the courage to ask one of my pseudo-relatives what we're waiting for. 'Patience, brother, patience.' I wish he hadn't said that. Don't say that to an anxious traveller.

Has Oge got cold feet? Am I to be jilted at the altar, or culturally pertinent equivalent?

Oge's womenfolk return. This time the guests applaud. Does this denote the last dance before the big moment? I bloody hope so. Oge breaks from the others and shimmies over to our table. She grabs my hand and leads me into the space between the clans. More applause. The music gets louder to the point of crackling distortion. 'Follow my moves!' she yells in my ear. My performance is about as graceful as anything Conor McGregor gets up to when not in the MMA ring. I can barely lift a foot without losing my balance. My arm movements are creepily jerky like a Ray Harryhausen model. I'm sure I spot a child recoiling from me with a quivering lower lip.

Not soon enough we're summoned to kneel before Dad, now sitting in a gaudy throne. My knees dig painfully into the stones on the ground. I try not to groan or wince, failing on the first count yet succeeding on the second. Dad blesses us in Igbo – wishing us a good home and many children, I'm told later – and touches our heads. This is it. We're married. No vows to exchange, no documents to sign.

I'm lifted. My lungs feel like they've been zapped with an industrial vacuum cleaner. The knots – no, the cables – in my stomach loosen then dissolve. All the booze I've necked is no longer simply watering down the edginess, it's been converted into carefree energy.

Now we must dance. Again. I don't overthink it. I don't think at all, in fact. I just move, which I believe is the point of the whole dancing shebang. I've no idea whether I look like a thoroughgoing wanker or not because I don't care. Not anymore. When I lean and bump and sidestep, Oge claps her hands and shouts, 'Ehhhh!' This can't be a bad sign, can it? After ten minutes of tripping the light fantastic – or the light adequate – my throat is shrivelling. Of course it is, I've spent the last five hours putting away nothing but alcohol in 36-degree heat. I groove over to a bottle of water under Dad's throne. Dad and some in-laws rubberneck me and clap their hands. Are they complimenting my moves or is this in fact a derogatory slow clap to be followed up with rotten tomatoes? I'd settle for the gesture to mean simply, 'We don't think you're a thoroughgoing wanker.'

18

There's no let-up in our social calendar. The following day is Dad's eightieth birthday. I'm at ease now so I'm looking forward to it. While consciously I didn't believe that the impending wedding was the source of my anxiety, perhaps unconsciously I did. When we arrive at the family home, the wedding marquee and tables still there, I let go and enjoy myself. I'm no longer seeing the world through piss-tinted glasses. Gone is the deadly tentativeness of yesterday. Today I listen closely to the 'high life' band that's been hired, realising that I prefer this genre to the ear-splitting Afrobeat that soundtracked our wedding. I have an appetite again, relishing each chomp of local, organic, homemade cuisine. I talk with great interest to my new relatives – pseudo and otherwise – and learn that my nephew is a budding rapper. He shows me a video he's made. His cadence and delivery are accomplished but I'm not sold on the lyrical and visual theme: making and spending masses of money. In one scene he snatches fistfuls of naira notes – I assume they're fake – from a steep pile.

His mum – my cousin – and a friend sit with us. They take it in turns to scold my nephew for not taking his college work seriously. If I was studying Business Administration and Office Practice, I wouldn't be taking it seriously either. I make an intervention that likely prompts my cousin to wish Oge and I a swift divorce. 'Follow your dreams, mate. You're an artist, that's your calling. If you study business practice or whatever then, sure, you'll get a job at the end of it. *Might* get a job. But will you be happy? Will your life have meaning? I tell you, when I was exactly your age I ...'

My cousin gathers up her robe and goes in search of a sick bucket, perhaps.

Oge's brother invites me into his wing of the house to meet some 'VIPs'. The opulent lounge is kitted out with gold-plated armchairs and an ivory-topped table strewn with Courvoisier and Cristal bottles. Below are Turkish carpets, above paintings of the places he's visited: pyramids in Egypt; ghats in Varanasi; the Leaning Tower of Pisa.

I'm introduced to a Cambridge-educated female lawyer from South Africa who used to be a politician in the ANC government. She hasn't heard of the university I work at but does compliment me for knowing a bit about South African literature. While we talk, she keeps bending her neck to look around me, perhaps at someone more interesting. 'I'll let you get on,' I sigh.

I get chatting with a fiftysomething Igbo couple originally from the next village but now based in Miami Gardens, Florida. Abel runs a chain of clothing stores while Jocelyn is a cardiologist. Between them they have a small property empire branching across the US, Canada, Nigeria, South Africa and the UK.

'You know, dude,' says Abel in a pitch-perfect African-American accent. 'Started out in London. Was driving cabs for close-on eight years. Done saved me enough bread to go Stateside, buy my first crib and all.' He offers me some Johnnie Walker Blue Label. 'Here on you don't need to ask, dude, just you be helping yourself to that.'

'Don't mind if I do, Abel.'

Oge glares at me from the midst of another conversation with her mum and a man with enormous, cymbal-sized hands who's a dead ringer for the actor Laurence Fishburne.

'We got some bottles of Macallan here too, wanna try?' asks Abel. 'They be different ages, you know.'

'This is very good, thank you.' I feel squiffy.

'I like all kinds, dude. What's good about being a man of means. Choice.' He leans towards me and lowers his voice. 'Truth be told, I can't tell the difference between the twenty-year-olds and the twenty-five-year-olds.' Abel chuckles. Jocelyn eyes him warily and sips Cristal.

'Are we still talking about whisky?' I ask.

Abel goes critical with laughter, drowning out all other interactions in the room for ten seconds.

Jocelyn takes up the conversational baton, although doesn't want to make eye contact with me. These days I never know whether this is a sign of contempt or neurodiversity or a bit of both – and how I should respond. She has more of a Nigerian accent than her hubbie, implying that she hasn't been away from the homeland as long. 'You are a college professor?' she asks.

'Mere senior lecturer.'

'Oh. And do you have a home in Igboland?'

'No. Do you?'

'We have three,' she says offhandedly, as if alluding to pairs of socks. 'I suppose before you came to Nigeria you thought we all lived in trees like monkeys.'

That feels like a stake in the heart. The insinuation that I'm racist, or at the very least idiotically unworldly, resurrects some dregs of anxiety from yesterday. I think hard about how to reply. I do so weakly. 'No, I used to work in Côte d'Ivoire. I've seen how people in Africa live.'

'Of course, Nigeria has a bad reputation internationally. We are thought to be criminals what with all the area boys – you know what they are?'

'Gangsters.'

'The area boys who seduce *your* old men and women on dating websites and defraud them of their life savings. And those emails from fake princes fishing for account details. I bet you did not know that many of those scams are perpetrated by people in *your* part of the world who pretend to be Nigerian.'

'I did actually.' I don't like Jocelyn's assumption that I'm totally ignorant because I'm white or Western. Moreover, I don't like the pronoun 'your' when I don't consider myself loyal to the people or places she mentioned.

'Did you drive here from Lagos?'

'We flew.'

'There is also scare-mongering about overland travel from west to east. The foreign media speak of bandits taking hostages, especially white ones, on those remote roads. Also, the Yorubas want the world to believe that going to Igboland is dangerous. But this is all sensationalism.'

Is she implying that, by flying rather than driving to Igboland, I've fallen for propaganda? 'I don't really know about that,' I say. 'I travelled here with my Igbo wife and as my Igbo relatives advised.'

Oge joins us – and not a moment too soon. 'Darling,' I say, 'meet Abel and Jocelyn. Abel's in business, maybe he can share some tricks of the trade.'

'Igbos be natural businesspeople!' proclaims Abel, clanging my glass with his.

'That is your last one tonight,' hisses Oge to me.

Abel's voice rises to comic falsetto. 'Come on, sister, he just gone got married. Dude's gotta celebrate.' He has another slug of whisky. 'First piece advice I can give is free: come to US. Got more Igbos there, so more of a network, right? I found in London a whole bunch of Yorubas and not so many Igbos. That makes business for our people harder, right sister?'

'One thing you *must* do,' says Jocelyn sternly, 'is be selective about who you befriend. Only connect with people of quality, people who are always moving forward in their lives. If you spend time with failures, then you, yourself, will fail.'

I pride myself on being able to get on with most human beings wherever they are in the world, but I draw the line at patronising and arrogant ones. And you find such twerps everywhere, if thankfully in small numbers.

Before Jocelyn can carry on, I say, 'Well, that's got to be my last drink. Let's go home.'

From Oge's expression I can tell that I'm about as convincing as an estate agent who harps on about the 'potential' of a property that's falling down around his ears.

19

Irritating as Jocelyn is, she's only that – an irritation. She will not floor me with a force ten storm wave of anxiety. The next morning, though, I'm tested at the breakfast table. Oge tells me that her aunt has complained about my 'drinking beer and just walking around all the time' and that a colleague of her brother's was perturbed by the amount of whisky I'd quaffed with him a couple of nights ago. His charge feels hypocritical – he was plying *me* with the liquor and downing shots, while I was at least savouring it.

'Is it worth telling them that I was drinking so much because I was anxious?'

'That is not something people understand here, *abi*.'

Oge's sister and my nephews join us. While the boys push each other at the breakfast cereal bar, she unburdens herself about woes she's had in Italy, where she lives. One of her boys was told that he was ugly by an Italian schoolmate. 'You don't belong here,' the schoolmate added for good measure. A week later, my nephew was the only child in his class not invited to another – also Italian – schoolmate's birthday party. My nephew is also the only Black child in his class.

'Would that happen in England?' Oge's sister asks me.

'I don't know. England, like the rest of Europe, isn't as enlightened as it thinks it is.' When I was in Côte d'Ivoire, I met people who'd suffered microaggressions in France, their former colonial ruler. One Ivorian told me that, after he landed his dream job working as an economist for the European Parliament, he went into his bank in Strasbourg to withdraw some money and was informed by the white manager that this was impossible. When asked why, the manager was evasive. Extra ID and immigration checks were necessary, he said. He interrogated my Ivorian friend about his travels, his education, his childhood. Only then would the bank manager give him access to his own cash. My friend's theory? 'Black people don't usually earn that kind of money, so they assumed I was a drug dealer.'

Jollier thoughts are triggered by Oge's decision to party this evening. It's New Year's Eve. The fun around the pool starts early. A band strikes up with instrumental covers of classic hip-hop and R'n'B numbers. Competing with that is karaoke at the other end of the yard. Food stalls, including a 'shawarma shack', spring up around us. By sunset folks are merry and dancing – if a little too close to the pool.

More relatives arrive, the younger ones taking the kids to bed. We occupy a large table, and I go to the bar. I ask for whiskies and Cokes and vodkas and lemonades. The barman places full-length bottles of those drinks on the bar.

'I want just single measures,' I shout over the noise. 'Please.'

'We only sell by the bottle, sir.'

'Is that normal?'

'It is normal in Nigeria, yes sir.'

'And some Nigerians have the neck to imply *I'm* an alcoholic?' I should have only thought that, but I said it out loud.

The barman swivels his head and shows me a cauliflower ear. 'Excuse me, sir?'

'Nothing. How much do I owe you?'

I get a round of applause when I return to the table with 750 millilitres of Johnnie Walker Red Label. Oge bear-hugs me and shouts, 'My n*****!'

My heart freezes. 'Did you just call me–'

Her sister-in-law points at me. 'Tom, you are a n*****! Yo, n*****!'

Oge whispers in my ear, 'It means something different here. Like you are a cool guy, a player.'

'Oh, right. Maybe don't say it when we're back in the UK. It'll be a hard one to explain.'

'It will be harder to explain if you call *me* n*****,' laughs Oge.

'If that was going to happen, I wouldn't be standing here now.'

The music stops. The countdown to midnight begins. Oge and I hold hands. 'Happy New Year!' the crowd exclaims in motley tones. Fireworks boom and crackle and lacerate the sky in the prettiest way.

20

Looking up at this extraordinary tree is like zooming in with a microscope to something deep and fundamental about reality. This might be due to the tight, twisting meshes of branches resembling the ladder patterns of the DNA helix that's at the core of all living organisms. Mostly I just have an overpowering feeling of awe as I stand under this emerald behemoth. I can understand why people might think it has magical properties.

'They say that when branches fall off the tree,' whispers Oge's brother, 'they never land on anyone below.'

Past the tree is a rumpled track that threads through pale, over-sunned farmland. Our SUV clunks across divots and depressions. The terrain is low and the sky barren enough for us to watch a distant storm, milky lightning prickling down from an onyx beret of cloud. It's a self-contained affair that plays out over a small patch of the boundless horizon.

We come upon a large property like my in-laws' up the road. It belongs to Chief Dr Chukwuemeka B Nweke, a well-regarded juju man. The steel gates in front of us are the size of castle turrets and are capped with CCTV cameras, suggesting that the chief doesn't entirely trust in the supernatural to safeguard his assets. I press a doorbell on the gates. We wait for a response. Our driver bangs the horn of the SUV. We're about to give up and go home when an old woman balancing an aluminium bucket on her head opens the gate for us.

We're taken into a courtyard and under a canvas-roofed gazebo. Inside are wickerwork chairs and a thigh-high table laden with gnarly chunks of white chalk and polyester flowers with non-precious jewels for stigmas. Two flunkies in polo shirts bid us to sit. The chief himself strolls out of the house wearing a coronet and furry loincloth. He sits on a throne at the head of the table. He's about thirty, athletically structured.

'Where from?' he asks me.

'UK.'

'I have people from UK come here. From Holland and Germany also.'

'What do they want?'

'Most have work and stress problems.'

'How do they find out about you?'

The chief clicks his fingers at his flunkies. They start filming him and me on their phones. 'I am on YouTube and Instagram. I have 87,000 followers on Facebook. I have five mobile phones.'

He prefers to tell me more in Igbo via Oge's brother, who kindly translates. Being a twenty-first-century juju, he frequently breaks off from our conversation to answer one of his quintet of phones. He says he gives his patients herbal medicines such as Alligator pepper, a cardamom-like spice which cures impotence. The effects are augmented by praying to one spirit or other in the animist pantheon. A common complaint is 'physical or spiritual illness'. When the chief describes the symptoms, they could be those of anxiety or depression: nausea; fatigue; headache; breathlessness. In such cases, the patient's ancestor has to be summoned in a ritual. This involves prayers, pouring libation onto the ground and marking the patient's head with a magical preparation that must remain secret. He picks up a piece of chalk, for these are used in rituals due to their pure and brilliant whiteness. Sacrifices are made of goats and fowl, for the spirits want to see blood. The chief says he once drowned a cow in a river to communicate with a patient's 'spirit wife'. Every human being is born with a spirit spouse which inhabits their placenta and is placed in a body of water after birth. It seems that animals and natural objects are manipulated to create a connection with the spirit world.

Graver illnesses demand a full-scale masquerade in which the juju man and his buddies wear masks that represent the spirits to whom they are appealing. These masquerades are accompanied by chanting, drumming and rattling. Men dance around waving dead birds' wings with animal pelts embedded with mirrors hanging from their backs. These objects, too, send a message to the supernatural plane. The chief points to a space-black tree encircled by empty bottles of liquor and decorated with the skulls of animals that, presumably, were sacrificed.

Often, the chief says, the spirit that inhabited the ancestor is a 'restless ghost'. It's stuck between the planes because the ancestor wasn't buried with the proper rites. I don't ask how this can apply to the Europeans he has treated, since their culture has different funerary practices. When the ancestor is re-buried symbolically with the correct rites the patient will be cured – that's the theory, anyway. The chief finishes by saying that juju healing comes with strings attached by the spirits. Insomnia could be the price of expanding your business, although I'd say there's a more scientific link between the conditions. At any rate, it seems Igbo animism has its version of the Faustian pact.

On the drive back to our hotel, Oge's brother says he's intrigued by Chief Nweke. As a businessman, he sees him through a commercial lens. 'There are not many juju men with an international client base.'

'Are you thinking of investing in him?' I ask, half-jokingly.

'I think I would invest in a documentary film about him. He is a one-off.'

'Let me know if you need a script.'

More enchantment is needed before Oge and I can fly back to Lagos. We drive through a village with an unsettling glut of wrecked cars on the edges of its main road. Just past a corrugated iron lean-to with vehicle parts hanging from its roof is Ogro Herbalism Centre, based in a wooden shack. Patients sit and wait on plastic chairs and benches outside it. A granny with an injured leg that hinges from the knee in the wrong direction leans on a Zimmer-type contraption made of four lashed-together walking sticks. From a house yonder comes American sports commentary. 'Wow, what a turn of events!' roars a Midwesterner at the peak of his voice.

While we wait Oge explains why we're here. The blessing we'll receive will either remedy a poison we might already have absorbed or protect us from one that could be chucked at us later. The first type is secreted in the food or drink of someone envied for their success, especially if they've made a life abroad.

'Is this very common?' I grimace.

'Common enough,' says Oge.

The second type of poison is administered with an invisible pin that flies through the air and pierces the skin. Both types of poison can cause fever and even death. For reasons unknown, as I've reduced my anxiety on this trip, so I've grown more agnostic. Why shouldn't I take all help potentially on offer whether it's traditional or modern, mystical or medical? May as well spread my bets.

We're called inside the shack. A young woman, perhaps a teenager, anoints my face with smoky-smelling oils, says some words in Igbo and tells me I'm fit to travel. She does the same for Oge.

'Is that it?' I ask Oge, expecting a more flamboyant procedure after hearing about Chief Nweke's exploits.

'You want to stay here until next Christmas?'

We hand over cash to an orderly on the way out.

'Job's a good 'un,' I say.

On the way to the airport, we get mired in another traffic jam, though nothing on the scale of Lagos. It's the fault of a man who's having to pick up planks of wood from the road and return them to the rear of his pick-up truck. For the last quarter of a mile, he was oblivious to the planks slowly spilling out of his truck as he drove. He's glaring and shaking as he goes about this miserable labour. I try to communicate with him telepathically: *May as well pray to the spirits, mate.*

My thoughts keep circling back to Oge's point about the power of belief. Whether or not there are ethereal beings that can be called on to rescue us from anxiety and other malaises, people all over the world *believe* there are. Is this that far from the anti-anxiety rituals I resort to without knowing whether physically or scientifically they are making any difference, from pacing around a hotel room to playing games on my phone?

The comic book creator Alan Moore says that magic is primarily about the human mind. Those fairytale sequences of a wizard casting a spell to heal or make someone sick – the Western equivalent of juju – can be understood as 'manipulating symbols, words or images to achieve changes in consciousness', as Moore puts it. The knock-on effects can be physiological, as I know from my own wars with anxiety when a bad frame of mind can speed up the heart and so on. We can use magic on ourselves, intentionally or not, and we can use it on others for good or for bad. 'An artist or writer is the closest thing you will see in the contemporary world to a shaman,' says Moore. 'Originally, all the facets of our culture, whether they'd be in the arts or the sciences, would be the province of the shaman. The fact that, in present times, this magical power has degenerated to the level of cheap entertainment and manipulation is, I think, a tragedy. At the moment, the people who are using shamanism and magic to shape our culture are advertisers. Rather than trying to wake people up, their shamanism is used as an opiate to tranquilise people.'

Normally I'd be cautious about mentioning a white writer from Northampton in relation to Nigerian spirituality, but Moore is a practising magician in a pagan tradition that has echoes of African animism. In fact, I find it reassuring that, once upon a time, folks all over the world largely believed in the same things: universal harmony; manifold deities; the power of nature and symbolism. It's a far cry from today's religious factionalism with Hindus against Muslims, Muslims against Christians, one type of Christian against another type of Christian and so forth ad infinitum.

21

Oge isn't her normal, sociable self as we sit with Chibuzo having an orange juice in our hotel bar. This is our last day in Lagos – and in Nigeria – and Oge is using it to catch up with old university friends. They're speaking in Igbo, so I can't fathom what's irking her.

When we've finished our drinks Oge announces, 'Let's have lunch, *O*.'

'We had it half an hour ago,' I protest. Not that I'm not hungry. I'm always hungry. But I can't just eat whenever I want.

Oge strolls out of the hotel, Chibuzo and I following. We go down an alley to a canteen. Working stiffs line up before steaming trays of stew and soup. Oge orders a takeaway box of the grub. She hands it to Chibuzo, who nods goodbye and disappears down the alley.

Oge kisses her teeth. '*Chai*, my pockets have run dry on this trip. Everybody wants to take something and you get to a point where you have nothing to give apart from what? Yourself? Your own body?' I guess this could be deemed expat anxiety, the obligation on those who move away to help the ones they left behind. It's a cursed kind of privilege that must make you question whether old pals are only still pally with you for a handout. And when new pals appear are they for real or just gold-diggers – or lunch-diggers?

'You know that some of my university mates have not had a single job since we graduated twenty years ago?'

I assume Chibuzo was one. I don't ask if we'll be meeting more of them tonight.

Smoke from a row of barbecues obscures the forty-inch screen showing Chelsea and Manchester United. It's as if the players are running around amid a riot that the police are dispersing with tear gas.

Zim is in a Chelsea shirt which ends a couple of inches short of his beer belly. He stands abruptly, bashing his knees against the wobbly table and almost knocking bottles of Gulder and Guinness over. He gives me a customary African handshake that starts with a thumb clasp and ends with a click of the fingers. I completely screw it up because I'm a foreign plonker. He calls to the waiter for more beer. He's on such a mission that he's spiking his own beers with sachets of ethanol that he buys from kids passing by with baskets of the stuff on their heads.

Oge and Zim catch up. I watch the football. We all eat some grilled fish. I drink a bit. Zim drinks a lot.

At 11pm I remind Oge that we have to be at the airport in a few hours.

'I will drive you,' Zim slurs. 'You are my guests.'

'Are you serious?' I gasp.

He looks hurt in that drunk, exaggerated way people look hurt when they're drunk.

'Really, Zim, it's okay. We'll get a taxi.' I really don't want to die in a pile-up in Lagos just after marrying the love of my life.

'Why will you not let me drive?' moans Zim.

'Because you've had seven bottles and God knows how many of those sachets.'

'Sweetie,' says Oge, 'Nigerians know how to drink and drive.'

'You mean it's not illegal?'

Zim can't conceal his grin with the back of his wrist.

'He's fine,' Oge insists.

The drive back seems quicker than the drive here. Maybe the roads are clearer or maybe Zim's so pissed he's flooring it. My guts are clenched throughout. I consider opening the door and bailing every time he leans over his shoulder to ask me a question about my job, the football team I support, what it's like in England.

'If you can keep your eyes on the road, Zim, I'll tell you whatever you want.'

I survived, or I wouldn't be writing this now. Later that morning, Murtala Muhammed Airport is a fraction of the hassle it was a fortnight ago. Is it objectively less busy or is my mood just chiller? A bit of both maybe. I don't want to be complacent, but when we land at Heathrow, I feel that maybe, just possibly, I've overcome some of my travel anxieties after weathering this high-pressure trip, which has changed my life for the better.

PART 4. FIVE TO FIFTEEN PER CENT

1

The lower third of the Edwardian terrace's decaying brickwork is disguised with white uPVC cladding that glares in the sun like the sight of a sniper's rifle in an action movie. The cinematic vibe extends to two security guards in combat trousers tucked into steel-toe-capped boots. They wear rectangular sunglasses that resemble the black strips placed over the eyes of people in sensitive photographs to protect their identities. They must be off-duty and work for another organisation – this country really has sunk to a new low if mental health providers now need private security.

I find Lauren in a nondescript office on the second floor. There's a refreshing absence of framed platitudes and new age bric-a-brac. Within moments of talking to Lauren – whose sensible bob, jumper and tweed skirt recall a primary faith schoolteacher – I can tell she's more authentic and better at her job than Jacqueline. In the counselling world, as in other areas of life, is it true that if you've got it you don't have to flaunt it – or try too hard to *appear* as if you know what you are doing?

She asks me questions and gives me time to answer them – an instant upgrade on Jacqueline. The most searching one is,

'What do you worry about consciously?' which is prompted by my confession that I don't understand what ails me subconsciously and how it erupts out of me as anxiety when I'm in an objectively peaceful situation.

'I worry about not being able to change,' I say.

'Change how?' asks Lauren.

'Eating better. Drinking less. Getting more exercise. Being more patient and kind to people.'

'What's stopping you?'

'Laziness, I suppose.'

'Sometimes we don't make an important change until it's too late – or almost too late.'

I think again of friends who died prematurely from their behavioural kinks. 'Do you mean like someone giving up the fags and pork pies after they have had a stroke?'

'If you want to put it like that.'

'That worries me too – not changing in time.'

'Some people are lucky in the sense that they receive a warning. It could be that stroke, to use your example, which wises them up and persuades them to lead a healthier life. But what if–'

'That stroke is fatal?' I finish her sentence for her.

'Exactly.'

I leave that session thinking hard about change. It's central to the anxiety puzzle. I think about what change requires of us, the sacrifices it demands. Bad habits that can cause unease – like too much booze and the wrong food – can take shape early in life and make 'pleasure pathways' in the brain that are hard to seal off or stray from in later life. Living with Oge reminds me of other compulsions that I took for granted when I was on my own and nobody noticed them: picking my nose; tearing the ends off my fingernails instead of clipping them; fidgeting (although that's a component of my anxiety, so you're cruel and prejudiced if you judge me for that – not that that's a defence in Oge's eyes).

'Maybe I can try to possibly make these changes when we go back to Nigeria,' I say to Oge, half-heartedly.

'How about take away the words "try" and "possibly"?' she replies. She hasn't known me long but she knows me all too well.

The next meeting with Lauren is equally productive. We talk more about how to switch behaviours, attitudes, values. Some of her ideas run counter to those of the psychoanalysts I cited earlier but that's okay – I'm happy to be a pluralist about method if it gets me better. I'm starting to see the point of counselling now. You just need a good counsellor, it seems.

2

Writing about travel can prompt anxiety. So can writing about preparing to travel. But you hope that once you've written about it there'll be catharsis, *Cambridge Dictionary* definition: 'the process of releasing strong emotions through a particular activity or experience, such as writing or theatre, in a way that helps you to understand those emotions'. In his discussion of the polymath John Ruskin, Alain de Botton bigs up the act of recording our travel experiences through writing or drawing: 'It [teaches] us to see – that is, to notice rather than merely look.' And the observant traveller will be more fulfilled, if they document things of beauty. 'In the process of re-creating with our own hands what lies before our eyes,' writes de Botton, 'we seem naturally to evolve from observing beauty in a loose way to possessing a deep understanding of its constituent parts and hence more secure memories of it.'

Where I'll fall down now is that I'm not going to reconstruct a beautiful moment. By rewinding my memories and referring to notes taken at the time, I'm focusing on an incident in 2024 that triggered mid-table anxiety. Maybe, though, if I'm anxious writing it, then the impact on you the reader will be anxiety-inducing, which has its virtues. Hunter S. Thompson remarked that the best way to appreciate his brand of 'gonzo' journalism was to get into the same mental space as he was when he wrote it, i.e. be as mashed on drugs as he was.

At the Nigerian High Commission, London, the burly security guard checks over my papers. 'Text is wrong in letter,' he says wearily. This can't be the first time he's seen this error.

My stomach tightens. 'How should it read, sir?' I ask, trying my damnedest to sound sanguine.

'Your wife wrote "I take full responsibility for my husband".'

'What should she have written, sir?'

'"I take full *immigration* responsibility for my husband".'

I want to challenge him. I want to ask him how often, in his experience, someone has sacrificed their good life in the UK to abscond to Nigeria and spend the rest of their days as an illegal immigrant selling feather dusters along the motorways. Of course I don't say this out loud. It would sound incredibly arrogant.

'What you should write is all there in the documentation,' says the security guard. He kisses his teeth while sneering into the middle distance. 'The documentation tells no lies. How far you come?'

'Two hours.'

'You don't want to go home, come back later?'

He's made me squirm. He should be satisfied. 'No, sir,' I murmur like a guilty schoolboy.

He points across the road to a corner shop. I go inside and find it profiteering from mistakes like the one I just made. Is the owner in cahoots with the High Commission? Between a column of canned chickpeas and a mini-fridge of reduced samosas is a PC and printer. For £2 I can correct one word in the letter – which, fortunately, I have in a folder on my phone – and print a fresh copy. I'm also liberated of £13.99 for a self-addressed and pre-paid envelope so that I can get my passport back, with visa inside – if I'm lucky.

Back at the High Commission, the attitude lurches from pedantry to laxness. Now forty minutes late for my appointment, the guard waves me in anyway. I sit down before a row of hatches, a soporific agent behind each. I'm called by a cherubic-looking guy of twenty. I hand him my papers. As he peruses the bank statements, I fear they look wonky and fake. They were produced by a funny little fax-like machine in my local branch. Yes, unbelievably for modern Britain, there's a branch of my bank that's within 600 miles of where I live. The clerk said that I'd have to wait until the end of the calendar month to get a more professional-looking statement. She didn't explain why. I didn't see the point in asking. These days I'm avoiding scraps with bureaucrats.

The cherub stashes my wedding certificate under his desk. *Do I get that back? Why is he taking so long over the bloody plane ticket now?* That's printed out poorly too because, well, I have a poor printer at home.

An anxious traveller is a vulnerable traveller. I'm ready for him to hold on to my wedding certificate and anything else he wants. I'm ready for him to charge me another £500 or £1,000. I'm ready for him to chloroform and gag me. As long as I get my bloody visa.

'Your outgoing flight is just two days after your incoming flight,' the man says neutrally, so neutrally that I'm suspicious. What does he want me to say – if anything – in my defence?

'We can … change … the ticket … later,' I whimper.

He nods sympathetically. Well, it looks sympathetic. 'You realise that, since this is your second visit to Nigeria, all this can be done online?'

'All this? All what?'

'Applying for your visa. You could have done it online. You didn't need to come here in person.'

3

At the travel clinic, the blue-bibbed pharmacist reads through the options for anti-malarial drugs. 'According to your records,' she says, 'you took Malarone last time.'

'Sounds right.'

'You said that you are prone to anxiety.'

'Yes.'

'Then I don't know why you were prescribed Malarone. Did you mention to the specialist last time about anxiety?'

'Pretty sure I did.'

'Well, let's put you on Doxycycline instead.'

'Yeah, I had that for three months in Côte d'Ivoire.'

'Did you suffer any anxiety then?'

'Not really.'

I know better than to ascribe my woes to this one factor. After all, I wasn't on any anti-malarial meds in either the Philippines or France and still fell foul of the fear.

If travel exposes you to new diseases then it can also relieve existing ones. Within seconds of stepping off the plane into 35-degree Lagos heat, I no longer feel the burn of the trapped back nerve that's been plaguing me in frigid England for two months. I'm reminded of a well-travelled friend, who's worked all around the planet as a schoolteacher, and his tales of his late mother. When she visited him in Muscat or Mexico City, she'd practically levitate in ecstasy because, at last, she was getting some respite from the rheumatism that dogged her daily in damp Dalton-in-Furness.

But my mind's straying into the trivial – no offence to my friend's mum – to avoid thinking about the serious purpose of this trip. We're here so that Oge can undergo in vitro fertilisation (IVF) in order that we, as oldish farts in our forties, can bring a baby into the world.

4

I'm young, a schoolboy again, but with an older head. Though I'm small and clutching a textbook and watching my peers flick bogies and fart at each other, I'm somehow aware that I've done all this before, that I've already been through school and college and university and a fair bit of adult life. And then the panic strikes. I realise I'll have to do all this all over again. All those GCSEs, those A-Levels, those degrees. I'm going to have to learn to swim and ride a bike. Again. Move to a new school and make friends. Again. Suffer alcohol poisoning. Again. Lose my virginity. Again. That first job interview. Again. Travelling for the first time to an alienating place. Again.

Then I wake up. This, too, is an anxiety dream. And it's happening more regularly now Oge and I are planning a family. It tallies with waking worries I have about putting someone through similar rites of passage. I recall the pain they caused me and wouldn't wish it on anyone else. The older I get the less sure I am that they were worth it – after these obstacles crossed, I'm still anxious and disillusioned and unsure of myself. I think others feel the same. It might be called 'getting older'.

This anguish is bolted on to the normal misgivings any new parent has. How do I hold the baby, should we get that far after our first round of IVF? How do I know if it's hungry, sick, too warm, too cold? To co-sleep or not to co-sleep? And if I had a pound for every time a prospective parent has told me that they're scared of bringing a child into a world that's going to the proverbial hell in a handcart, I'd have enough dosh by now to build Junior a subterranean nuke-proof bunker in the American Redoubt. Whereas in the past the existential threats were exaggerated, now Ragnarok's in sight unless humankind gets its shit together fast. When the young 'un's thirty, will she have to forage for scraps of food in blistering heat in a desertified Hampshire – or an endlessly flooded one à la *Waterworld* – while being shot at by eye-patched *Mad Max*-esque vigilantes? Or, if I can't get the bunker made, will she have to stagger around in a nuclear winter amid the rubble and the ash clouds? This isn't idle speculation – the Doomsday Clock is closer now to midnight than ever before, even at the height of the Cold War.

Then there's the disquiet about bringing up a mixed-race child in a society that's taken several cranky, wheezy steps back from tolerance. Last Christmas, a friend of Oge's and her daughter came over for dinner. The daughter had had some aggro in secondary school. She said nonchalantly, 'A white boy punched me in the stomach and called me a n*****.' Her mum said that the school didn't take their complaint seriously. The headteacher advised the family to 'build resilience'. Hearing this sent me into a tailspin. The simple injustice of this incident was bad enough, but the effects could be lifelong, causing someone to lose both their sense of self-worth and any chance of integrating into a society that's structured to spurn them. People of colour have to endure this bollocks all the time. I don't want that for my little person of colour.

5

I must park these thoughts for this second trip to Nigeria. De Botton's technique of writing and observing allows me to stay in the present. I plan to remain anonymous, to fade into the background in my sunglasses and not say a word unless spoken to first. Often enough, nobody wants to speak to me anyway. There isn't the same reverence here for Westerners as in other parts of the non-West. I tan easily so perhaps people don't know how to place me racially or culturally. In Côte d'Ivoire, after a few weeks in the blazing sun, I earned the sobriquet 'demi-blanc'. This did me no favours – some Black Ivorians thought I was Lebanese, an ethnic group many of them resent. They're seen as exploitative of Black Ivorians.

I don't mind being ignored. It takes the pressure off.

My approach is rewarded with a softer ride at Murtala Muhammed Airport compared to last time. With few travellers around, there are no long waits or public disturbances. 'Nobody is here because they cannot afford to visit home,' says Oge. 'Blame *your* cost-of-living crisis.'

In-country Oge does all the talking – and all the doing. If this sounds like an unfair division of labour, she won't have it any other way, especially as, when I try to negotiate the price of a taxi, I end up costing us twice as much as it should. She calls me a 'useless man'. It prompts me to think about generations of British – and probably men of other nationalities – who came before me, who couldn't cook, clean, iron or dress themselves without the assistance of women: mums; grannies; aunts; girlfriends; wives. Walking down the street, we hold hands in a way that feels maternal, as if I'm a kid again not wanting to lose sight of his mum in the supermarket. We've never been closer, and I've never felt more certain about my relationship with another human being. We're on a mission here to make a baby. Not much else matters.

The streets drip with danger: potholes; heaps of rubbish; broken glass; channels of acrid green water conveying disease. Cars and motorbikes speed past, no pavements for protection. But I'm gliding through it, noting what's enticing about this urban salmagundi. While Oge buys phone credit from a vendor – everything's a negotiation – I gaze at the coconut husks and shards of tiles slotted between bricks in the pavement. The intention is practical, to stop people tripping in the gaps. But for me there's a collage aesthetic – beauty in necessity. Black polythene bags blow around the ground at such a slow, intermittent pace that, when caught in the corner of the eye, they can be mistaken for skulking rodents. High above them, the spirals of barbed and razor-wire shielding properties are like curl-cuts of butter at a swanky dinner. I'm pulled out of my reverie by Oge asking the saleswoman, 'Are you okay?' This is the third top-up card she's tried and the credit's not appearing on her phone. She's interrupted by a booming Tannoy announcement: 'Eliminate all sexual frustrated infections!'

If we can't make our phones work, then we'll at least withdraw money and avoid starvation. That's no breeze either. We traipse up a main road, enter the first bank we come across. I try my card in the ATM. It's spat out before I've fully inserted it. I ask the clerk why and she says, 'Foreign cards not valid.'

'Are they valid in other banks?'

'I don't think so, sir.'

'Transfer money into my account and I will withdraw for you,' says Oge. Easier said than done too. Even with a Nigerian card the maximum you can take out in a day is 5,000 naira (about £2.50). This won't go far. 'Do not dice with the machine,' says Oge. 'If it swallows your card you will have to write a letter and go through a formal process to retrieve it. We cannot go through that.'

On to the next bank. That cultural theme that started to reveal itself on my first visit to Lagos – official propriety sabotaged by technical dodginess – has its apogee in this branch of the Fidelity Bank Nigeria. We're patted down by pistol-hipped guards before going through a double-doored security entrance. The first door opens automatically, allowing us into a tiny cubicle, but the next door that leads into the bank doesn't. Are we in shtuck? Have we become unknowing fugitives and will be stuck in this claustrophobic space until the police arrive? Oge and I have to squeeze up against each other for five minutes while a guard grits his teeth and tugs open the exit door with his fingers.

Oge joins a queue the length of Andrew Tate's rap sheet. I offer to stand with her in solidarity, but she orders me to a seat. I try to plug my phone charger into a socket on the wall. The socket has been badly made, so the charger won't fit. I carry on reading Chimamanda Ngozi Adichie's autobiographical novel *Purple Hibiscus*. I reach a scene in which the animist grandfather of the heroine Kimberly announces that the white Christians he has met must be insane because they believe that their God and his son are one and the same thing. I won't be sharing that with Oge the Roman Catholic.

Forty-five minutes later, Oge comes over to me, face elongated. 'Imagine! They have only 20,000 naira on the whole premises. They have a vault and security guards, but only 20,000 naira. They are surely making jest. This country is so fucked up.' Oge seldom swears. She must be fed up.

We've spent most of an afternoon failing to obtain chump change. We have nary enough cash for the taxi home, which rising heat and flagging energy levels demand. Outside the bank a female security guard with a flat-top starts to usher us to a taxi. An old timer with a disarrayed beard steps in our way. 'What are you doing out of your post?' he shouts at the guard.

'Excuse me, uncle,' says the woman, 'I am serving these people.'

'I am not your uncle,' says the man. 'And that is not your post. *I* am a taxi driver and *I* will serve them.' He thrusts a sovereign-ringed finger at the bank. 'Return to your post, young girl.'

This strikes me as oppressive. I'm angry rather than anxious, but I know that both feelings come from the same destructive source and could have the same destructive outcome. But it's not my place to intervene. That'll go down like an avalanche of foie gras at a veganism festival. Clocking that I might do something moronic, Oge tells the man to get lost. He refuses to. She tells him again and adds that under no circumstance will she and her husband hire his cab. He duly gets lost.

6

It's a tribute to globalisation that St Ives Fertility Clinic, Lagos, looks and feels like any other half-decent medical facility I've been to anywhere in the world. The walls and tiled floors are radiantly white. The doctors and nurses are in white too and stride up and down the corridors with reassuring purpose. Pan pipe renditions of *The Godfather* theme tune and Celine Dion songs play low on speakers, intended to soothe. They cause me minor infuriation. The citrus-scented air freshener is a little too chemical for me. Still, it beats the stench of particulates outside.

What's different here from other facilities is the six-foot-tall oblong air conditioner that makes a sound like an old man choking on his own vomit. The other clients are well-dressed whereas I'm in sweat-stained shorts and an off-white T-shirt fraying at the neck. Why should I care, though? I'm a paying customer like everyone else. Oge would disagree – and not politely. She's fond of telling me that Nigerians are persistently baffled as to how Westerners can be so rich yet so scruffy. Here, only menial workers wear shorts. The poorest people stuck in slums nonetheless bother to don smart shirts and dresses – and bother to iron them. It's called having pride, apparently.

As we wait for our appointment, I notice a man in a turquoise suit with sleeves rolled up to mid-elbow gripping his head. Is he fretting about nurture versus nature, about the egg donor passing down awful habits? The clinic only screens for physical defects. Is he bricking it as hard as I am over the sorry odds of coming away from here with a bun in the oven?

My eyes waft away from him and on to others in the room. I register that Oge and I are the only mixed race couple present. I mention this to her.

'Why does that surprise you?' she replies.

'I thought we wouldn't be the only ones based abroad to take advantage of the cheap IVF.'

'There are not so many marriages between Nigerians and Westerners these days. I told you before about the misgivings we have.'

'Oh, yes. The mental illness and sex stuff.'

'There are other reasons.'

'Really?'

'They say that you smoke cigarettes so that you can stay warm in your cold countries. They say that you are white because–' Oge breaks off into laughter for a moment. 'You are white because you are ill. Like you are lacking vitamins. Or you are on the brink of death. Or you are ghosts.'

'Alright, love, I get the message. I didn't have a choice about the skin I was born with.'

All of which reminds me, again, of Côte d'Ivoire. My photographer colleague Alex Sebley – who is positively Aryan in appearance – and I would rock up to some village and all the children would start crying. It took a particularly candid dad to inform us that the only white people the kids had met before were doctors from aid organisations who'd shoved vaccine needles in them.

Before this chat can get any more uncomfortable, we're called in to meet our doctor. We sit for a while in an empty office with a hospital bed in it. From somewhere comes the smell of delicious savoury food. A granny grins at us from a poster. The caption reads: 'Sixty-seven years of age – oldest successful IVF patient in Africa.'

'I guess she had her treatment done here,' I muse.

'They would not advertise a rival clinic, would they?' says Oge. 'I heard that another lady came here and had triplets. She was 55 and had already entered the menopause.'

'People come away with more children than they bargained for. We'd settle for one, wouldn't we?'

'I have always wanted four.'

'First things first, dear.'

A towering doctor with a vast bald head like a planet strides into the room and takes a seat. A much smaller nurse follows him in. She casually hops up onto the bed and sits on it, legs dangling.

'Who are you, please?' the doctor asks.

Oge kisses her teeth. 'The lady out there gave us forms which we filled out. She took the forms and should have given them to you.'

'Don't worry,' he says, 'the forms will come.'

'They should have come already. That is not good, not encouraging.'

The doctor holds his hands up. 'Do you have your test and scan results?'

'We have some from the UK and we are waiting for some more here.'

'How old are you, missus?'

'Forty-three.'

He looks to me. 'And you, sir?'

'Forty-four.'

'How long have you been married?'

I don't see the medical relevance of that question but tell him anyway. 'Eighteen months.'

Another nurse arrives with our forms. The doctor pores over them. His eyes shoot up to meet Oge's. 'The issue we have is your thyroid.'

'I've been on medication for it for some time now.'

'You have a hormone imbalance. This test from England says so.'

'Yes, but I want to use an egg donor.'

'That is okay.' The doctor goes back to the form. 'You have one growth of fibroid inside. We will scan that again tomorrow and see if it will be a problem.'

Oge points to me. 'My husband is only here for a brief time, so we want to know when he can give you his sperm.'

'We will have to analyse it. If it is usable we will freeze it.'

I can feel the dread bubbling in the lower intestine. 'How many times will I have to, er, make a deposit?'

'Only once, we hope. If the first sample is not usable, we will ask you to do it again. If necessary, would you be able to come back in a few weeks to give more?'

'Not really, as I need to be back to work in the UK in the next fortnight.'

'That is okay also.'

'Can I give you a deposit today?'

'When last did you make love?'

Sadly, this has not been a priority of ours lately and, to my embarrassment, I can't remember. 'It was last week,' says Oge.

The doctor peers at me, man-to-man. 'When last did you ejaculate, sir?'

My eyes plummet to the floor. 'About a week ago.'

The doctor nods. 'Can you make love today?'

'Right now?'

Everyone laughs apart from me.

'No, sir, when you get home.'

'Why do we have to make love today?' asks Oge.

'Your husband needs three days of abstinence before making the deposit on Thursday.'

'But I've had a week of abstinence already,' I say.

Oge raises a finger to catch our attention. 'We should mention that my husband has had some irritation down there when he pees–'

'I don't think that's serious,' I interrupt.

'We should mention it,' Oge insists. 'And there is a redness to it.'

The doctor stands up and walks over to the bed. The nurse gets off it. 'Can you come here please, sir?' I join him and he draws a linen curtain around the bed. He asks me to pull my trousers down and lift my penis up so he can see it.

'There is some trauma on the glans,' the doctor says.

'I don't know why. I haven't touched it for a week.'

'It looks like a bruise. We can give you antibiotics.'

'Is it infected?'

'No, no, no.'

'Then why take antibiotics? You only need antibiotics if there's an infection, right?'

'It is a precaution against infection.'

The doctor returns to his desk, reaches down to a cupboard and retrieves an open polystyrene box of jollof rice.

7

I awake from another anxiety dream. It's 4am in Oge's brother's house in Ikeja, Lagos. Oge and I and our sheets are one big sweaty mess. There's a power cut so there's no air con. It's too expensive to run the generator all the time. Since I won't get back to sleep, I write down what I recall of the dream. Two emaciated prisoners were being marched through the snow at gunpoint. Some kind of war was on. They weighed up the odds of escaping or not. If they made a run for it they might get shot. Or the guards might not bother wasting bullets on them. If they didn't run they might die of hunger or overwork in the concentration-camp-type place they were being herded to. Or they might survive it and see their families again when the war finished. I try to decipher the dream and can't get beyond banalities. Is it that I'm facing a Hobson's choice? That all next possible steps could unleash anxieties? If the IVF fails then we return home distraught and have to dredge up all reserves of willpower to go through the bloody thing all over again.

5–15. These digits are etched in my mind. This is the percentage chance of IVF working first time for women aged over 40. 5–15 per cent. When I first read it, I was ready to sack the whole thing off. Oge, the eternal bright-sider, won me over. We've talked this through. We're steeled for disappointment. But supposing we succeed on this cycle or the next or the next, then I'll be back to worrying about bringing a child into a rotten world. I'm worrying about it already and it isn't even a prospect yet.

8

On paper, there's plenty to be anxious about on this trip, but I'm managing not to feel anxious. I'm not sure why and to analyse it might jinx me. What is unsettling me, though, is the way middle-class Nigerians treat the poor. This includes Oge. I don't want to raise it with her. I might be taken as churlish and naive and oblivious to the gigantic pressure she's under. In my experience, there are certain people who never want to lead or take responsibility for activities involving two or more people but will be the first to criticise whoever does step up to that role. Is it a variant on the 'back-seat driver' trope? I don't want to be that guy, certainly not towards my wife.

Nonetheless, my discomfort grows every time Oge interacts with our 'houseboy' Femi. He's employed by Oge's brother to look after the property when it's vacant and to serve as a general dogsbody when it's occupied. At night he sleeps in a shed, by day he's at our beck and call. Oge will click her finger and yell, 'Femi, fetch Tom some beers.' Femi will duly go to one of the street stalls that's encased by an anti-theft cage with sachets of tomato purée and ethanol hanging off its bars. Or she'll tell him to turn on the generator or open the vehicle gate or sweep the front yard. My objections are myriad: it's a demeaning job; the poor lad never seems to go home to see friends or family; he's probably paid a pittance; everybody patronises or shouts at him and nobody ever says 'please' or 'thank you'.

I fret that repressing my concerns might morph into anxiety. This comes to a head when we buy some vegetables from an eight-year-old girl on the street. When the haggling is over, the girl doesn't have a plastic bag – called a 'nylon' here – big enough to hold our purchases.

'Why do you not have the correct size?' Oge snaps at her. 'Why do you not think about this before you come out to sell?'

The girl's lips fasten. She holds the too-small nylon up like a shield against the censure.

'Young girl, you are not prepared well,' Oge adds.

I unzip my backpack. 'Steady on, love, we don't need a nylon. We don't want to generate extra waste anyway.'

'This is not good, O.'

I smile at the girl. 'She probably doesn't have any choice over the size of the nylons she's given. Look at her, she's only a kid.' I load the avocados, tomatoes and bitter leaves into my backpack. This achieves détente by making the argument about how to get our shopping home redundant. I haven't offended Oge by questioning her rough treatment of the girl and the girl has been spared further rough treatment. And I can stop feeling anxious about it all. Not a bad outcome all round.

Whether this near-falling out with Oge makes any difference or not, it seems from then on that Femi is treated better. Each day Oge offers him a portion of whatever she's cooking for lunch and dinner. When he brings me beer, I insist that he has one for himself. When we go out in the evening, we tell him he can go and see his family or mates or do whatever he likes. He's so loyal to the household that I'm not sure he takes up the offer.

9

'Are you for Israel or Palestine?' asks the bookshop owner.

I look down to a bootleg copy of *No Longer At Ease* by Chinua Achebe and flick through the pages. They have the flimsy, slippery texture of old-school fax machine paper. The text is poorly reproduced – half the paragraphs on each page are so faint as to be illegible.

'Sir, Israel or Palestine?'

I'm ignoring him because it's not worth getting into a debate about the Gaza genocide in a city that's flying so many Star of David flags. 'I'm completely against what Israel are doing to the Palestinians,' I say eventually.

'I am wholly for the Israelites because I am Igbo and they are my ancestors.'

'So were some of mine.' I gesture to Oge who's on the shop's threshold. 'And so were hers. But that doesn't mean we have to support everything the modern state of Israel does, right?'

'I think it does.'

I contemplate telling him that, by his logic, every ethnically British person should support everything Keir Starmer does or Boris Johnson did, and that he and all *his* people ought to be full-square behind every corrupt Igbo baby-kisser going. Instead, I ask, 'How much do I owe you for the book?'

Outside, Oge commends me for 'handling the situation well'. She adds with a giggle, 'Maybe my husband is learning to be a diplomat at last.'

We catch a cab to the Lekki district of Lagos and look around the splendid Nike Gallery (no relation to the global sportswear brand). The receptionist tells me that an American politician called Lincoln dropped by a few months ago.

'Lincoln?' I check.

'Yes, sir.'

'That would be an achievement. He died in 1865.'

The man takes me over to a cargo crate half-filled with framed paintings. He flicks through them and pulls out a ropey portrait of Antony Blinken, the current US Secretary of State. Why so ropey? The artist's sympathies might lie with the Palestinians.

On the way home, with Gaza still on my mind, we witness a war-zone-like scene. Nigerian military policemen in camouflage are swarming around an SUV with 'PRESS' written on its passenger door. The policeman nearest the vehicle is remonstrating with the driver so passionately that his beret teeters on his head. We don't get to see what comes of this, not that we want to. We have the privilege of just passing by.

10

'Is he high?' whispers Oge to me, as our taxi driver skims the backside of a pedestrian wearing – improbably – a Bonzo Dog Doo Dah Band T-shirt.

'Love, are you with me?' Oge hisses.

I'm too preoccupied with wondering how the chuffing hell a twenty-year-old Nigerian in 2024 gets hold of a T-shirt referring to an obscure experimental British rock band from the 1960s. 'Sorry, love, we know what Lagos taxi drivers are like, don't we?'

I'm trying to put a brave face on it, but I can feel that horrid strain in the lower right abdomen. My palms and armpits are clammy. I aid my swallowing with a slug of bottled water. I start to notice a potent smell of petrol. I slide into the chicken-and-egg loop: am I feeling ill because of fumes coming from the petrol or am I feeling ill because I'm worried about the fumes from the petrol – and does it matter either way? The point is, I feel awful.

Oge reaches forward and taps the back of the driver's headrest. 'Is there a leak here somewhere? This smell is not good, O.'

The man shrugs and shakes his head. 'No, aunty.'

Oge kisses her teeth. 'Did you refuel before you picked us?'

'No, aunty.' He's not going to own that and risk losing a customer, such is the ruthless rat race of late capitalism. I don't blame him.

'It is quite horrible, isn't it?' I whisper. I instantly regret it. Now Oge might feel responsible for me. I don't want to add to her burden.

As if the petrol reek wasn't bad enough, I can also smell burnt plastic. I don't know whether my mind is playing tricks. I open my water bottle and realise that this new smell is coming from that same bottle. Am I drinking something toxic? I know I'm already inhaling oodles of pollution, since Lagos was recently ranked 123rd in a 'world's most polluted cities' survey by IQAir. 'Every day,' the report found, '227 vehicles clog each kilometre of road. Most of these vehicles are over fifteen years old and are not equipped with the latest emission technologies. The fuel they use has a very high sulphur content which is 200 times higher than U.S. standards for diesel.' The survey included data on over 5,000 cities, with New Delhi deemed the unhealthiest. Lindenberg im Allgäu in Germany was the healthiest, probably because it's 800 metres above sea level and is nested in forests and fields.

I want leave of my constricted car seat. That can't be done without bailing out into a Lagos motorway and getting myself flattened.

Thankfully, we reach the clinic before hardcore panic hits. The anxiety dissipates the moment I step out of the car.

An hour later, I'm sitting half-naked on a tungsten-hard bed in what looks like a budget hotel room. It is in fact a room in the St Ives Fertility Clinic where I must produce my sperm sample. I look down at my limp, unaroused member and say to myself, *At least I feel better now than I did in that bloody car.* That's one advantage to being an anxious traveller: the randomness of when and where the fear will strike is such that potentially humiliating and lonely situations that might reasonably produce fear – like this one – don't produce fear … if you're lucky.

11

When the deed is done, we stop in at a grocery store near the clinic. We want to buy Nigerian foodstuffs not least because they are infinitely tastier than their UK counterparts. Avocados, for example, are rich, creamy comestibles that bear no relation to the shrivelled monstrosities that you buy in a Britannic bodega that are harder than Benjamin Netanyahu's heart and which require a sledgehammer and a gallon of olive oil and 68 different spices in order to convert them into the middle-class pseudo-delicacy known as 'smashed avocado'. Eggs, too, are supernaturally delicious here when compared to the bland avian abortions Blighty-side. Local tomatoes taste of … tomatoes, rather than like crunchy, watery ping pong balls. Perhaps the only positive payoff of British colonialism in Nigeria – from the perspective of the formerly colonised, at least – is that classic British snacks like meat pies and Scotch eggs, when given a Nigerian twist, taste a damn sight better than the originals they were based on. They're the opposite of parodies, the imitations bettering the originals.

Yet, in this particular shop, we find none of the above. Instead, there are goods that you would normally find in a poncey Western health food shop but for even more stratospheric prices. I eye up a jar of cashew nuts and calculate that it costs the equivalent of £34 – no word of a lie. How can they justify that? Cashews are indigenous to West Africa. Are they sprinkled with gold dust? Laced with cocaine? Does each jar come with the deeds of a stately home? I read the small print and learn that the company behind the exorbitant savoury fruit in question is based in Vermont, USA. So, to get this straight: produce that can practically be picked off trees for free round here has been imported from over there with massive tariffs applied. Naturally, I pull out my phone to take a picture of the price tag. The cashier storms over to me and says, 'You cannot photograph, sir.'

'Why not?'

'No photographs allowed, sir, just purchases.' Now her lips are quivering. She looks to be on the cusp of tears. I don't want to ruin someone's day over a handful of pre-dinner snacks. I fling my phone back into my pocket and assume that other Western imbeciles have come here before and posted piss-taking pics of this shop's overpriced wares on social media … and are heading for hell at high-speed as a result.

The naira Oge spent on several phone top-up cards has proven to have been a criminal waste of money, since she can't summon the mobile data to book a taxi home. We find a Western-style café that sells the depressingly familiar overpriced mugs of milky froth with a dash of coffee added, alongside local spins on Western culinary themes that were manky in the first place, such as 'egg, bread and cold baked beans'. At least

I learn a new Nigerian-English verb: *to mise*. This is derived from the noun 'miser', as in someone who's averse to spending money at all costs – apart from the cost of one's self-respect and the respect of everyone else. Oge asks the waitress if she can please borrow her phone for a few seconds to arrange a cab. Fishily quickly – indeed before Oge has finished asking the question – the waitress tells us that she definitely doesn't have enough load on her phone.

'She is just mising,' growls Oge, not quite out of the waitress' earshot.

'What are we going to do? Walk?'

'Nobody walks in Lagos unless you want the Grim Reaper at your door.'

'What are we going to do, sleep in this booth?' My ever-anxious head time-travels back to ill-planned student expeditions to drum 'n' bass clubs in the late nineties/early noughties – the era I have to thank partly for my current malaise, given the rather large quantity of drugs consumed. In those days I was quite prepared to sleep in train stations, bus stops, the backs of taxis, the passenger seats of friends' cars, the chill-out rooms of nightclubs and even mini-skips. Now I'm supposed to be better than that, what with a child hopefully on the way and my being very much the wrong side of 40 years old.

12

I discover the equivalent of a local pub in our neighbourhood. It's called a 'spot' and comprises some plastic chairs, a barbecue and a lean-to with a fridge full of Gulder and Heineken beers under it. The owner calls himself Jeff, which I don't believe is a traditional Nigerian name. He sits down next to us and proudly announces that his first-born daughter is studying in a London further education college. Jeff made his money as a second-hand car dealer in Munich. He happens to be Igbo, so he and Oge exchange words in their language.

'Come tomorrow, *ogo*,' he says to me. *Ogo* means in-law in Igbo, I've learned. 'Enjoy barbecued chicken with me.'

'Thank you.'

On the stroll home, Oge voices concerns. 'Why are you making friends with just any old person here?'

'Just trying to be friendly, dear.'

'You do not know if he is sincere.'

'Well, he was kind and invited us back tomorrow. I was just trying to be kind back to him.'

I get a judgy silence in return. I don't say anything else. I try to figure out why she might be suspicious. When I lived in the Philippines in 2009–10, my local friends would occasionally inform me that they had met another Briton and that I ought to hang out with them. I always demurred because the last thing I wanted to do was come all that way to hang out with some right-wing geriatric expat with a Filipina girlfriend young enough to be his granddaughter. Maybe Oge's thinking is similar.

At the house, I pick up on some clues as to Oge's resistance. 'Some Igbos are useless men. If he has family members in Germany and England and wherever, he might have abandoned them there.'

'Is there a chance he's a nice man?' I venture.

Oge sighs in a way that suggests that there's a complex tangle of thoughts and feelings about the matter that, as a foreign greenhorn, I'll never understand. 'Igbos often relocate abroad,' she explains. 'They start businesses and families in Europe or the Americas. Let me tell you about my friend who went to Brazil. She raised a family there and started to miss home later in life. It is every Igbo's desire to one day return to the homeland. My friend also wanted to live more cheaply. Land is cheaper here. Living is cheaper here. A week before she was due to come back to Nigeria for good, she died in a car crash. It was like God was stopping her from coming home.'

'That's tragic,' I reply. 'But Jeff doesn't fall into that category, does he?'

'He might belong to another group who return here because they have failed over there. They might have committed a crime there and run back home.'

I hate to be influenced by stereotypes, but when someone – whatever their class, creed or colour – tells you that they were once a second-hand car dealer, it's hard not to think of grand theft auto or a showroom going up in flames for an insurance scam.

'So just be careful about who you make friends with here,' Oge warns as we climb into bed.

I fall asleep wondering how drunk or anxious or just plain crazy I'd have to be before I entered into a business transaction with Jeff. I was just hoping for a juicy chicken dinner tomorrow.

13

Why is it that, no matter how hard I try to book a flight that leaves at a reasonable time, I always find myself getting up at an obscene hour in order to make aforesaid flight? As I shower and dress while trying not to wake Oge, my chest feels tight and thick. It's not painful, just annoying, distracting. It's been like this for a couple of days and has meant an unhappy end to an otherwise successful trip, both in terms of what Oge and I came here to do and my own wellbeing.

Out the taxi window, under the blushing lights and ad hoardings suspended in the darkness, I see two guys squatting in the back of a moving refuse truck. Lagos is truly the city that never sleeps – or many Lagosians never sleep, such is the perpetual need to hustle. As I leave this megalopolis for a second time, my awe is inspired by its scale and busyness and buzzy audacity. Big cities in the Global North pale in comparison. Although they were once the models that the Global South followed, often intentionally through colonial architecture and design, now they 'are being dwarfed and prettified', argues the British travel writer Sam Miller. 'It's the new and ancient cities of Asia that are the pulsating giants of the twenty-first century.' I would humbly add African cities to Miller's list.

My flight of fancy crunches onto the runway of realism. I'm back to the chest-block and laboured breathing. My twin adversaries, car travel and having to stay seated, are temporarily eluded when I jump out of the taxi with my luggage. I hold them at bay with a beer in the departure lounge. It's 5.14am, but when you're travelling it's okay to booze at that time … isn't it?

There's some respite as I board the plane. But as soon as I sit down in my cramped mid-row seat, two large people – even larger than me – on either side, the fear floods back in.

'Do not shake your leg next to mine!' complains the trad-gowned Yoruba woman sitting to my left.

I'm already fidgeting and I haven't realised. I'm counting on her not to construe it as assault. I have the explosive urge to rise and stand in the aisle. I can't do that – we're about to take off. I close my eyes, try to wrest control of my breathing. *Calm. Calm. Calm.* Not working. I look up, imagine I have superhero X-ray vision. I see into my backpack stashed in the overhead compartment. I see the Propranalol packet. Unopened, unused.

We take off, ascend. I nudge the guy to my right, who's already fallen asleep. He awakes sluggishly and squeezes into his seat so I can slip past. 'Sorry,' I say too many times. I stride to the galley. A flight attendant snaps up straight from being bent over removing trays from their compartments. 'Sir, we will bring the drinks trolley soon.'

I stride back up the aisle. What's the betting that, based on this behaviour, they think I'm already drunk and won't serve me? My neighbour's asleep again, so I have to wake him again. I turn on the in-flight entertainment and watch a film called *The Royal Hotel* about two young women backpackers who get work in a redneck bar in the Australian outback. If you haven't seen the movie, you can guess that it all goes horribly wrong for them.

It's going horribly wrong for me, too, despite my regular trips to the galley to collect cans of beer and tumblers of whisky. Towards the end of *The Royal Hotel*, with four hours of my flight still to endure, the simple act of inhaling oxygen and exhaling carbon dioxide becomes as hard as ziplining in a suit of armour. My head's whirling. I've got brutal indigestion. My extremities have gone numb. I come crushingly close to begging for help from the flight attendants. I won't receive any *real* help from them. They're not medically trained, they can't dispense drugs. But my agitated soul is angling for reassurance that someone cares.

It's just as well that I don't do that. The poor guy next to me, whom I've disturbed no fewer than five times so far, would be within his rights to pelt me to death with all the Brewdog cans strewn around my tray table.

As soon as I step from the plane's gangway into Heathrow, my lungs are my own again. The fear's been supplanted by the early signs of a cold. I'll take a tickly nose and sandpapery throat any time. I breeze through arrivals, wait for the machine to fart out my luggage and make it out into the coach station.

It's as if the last six hours of anxiety never happened. But this is part of the problem of why my anxiety keeps returning – I'm so relieved when it's gone that I don't do enough work while I'm feeling alright to avoid relapsing. Worse, I revert to bad habits – like drinking – that will only trigger the heebie-jeebies all over again.

Not this time, though. While Oge stays on in Lagos to have the embryos implanted in her and receive hormone treatment, I reduce my drinking. I'll have to find other ways to insulate myself against the nerve-racking wait to find out if we can join the elite 5–15 per cent of first-time IVFers.

My nerves are racked in a bipolar way. It's good news one day, bad news the next. By the time Oge flies back to the UK, one out of the three embryos has survived and is growing. The first test she takes here shows low hormone levels. Then they improve. Then she does another load of tests and we're called in to talk to our GP. He informs us with a mile-long face that our pregnancy is 'unsafe'.

'What does that actually mean?' I ask.

'This pregnancy has a 20 per cent chance of success.'

Hand-in-hand, Oge and I slope out of the surgery devastated. My reaction is not that of agitation. It's slow-motion melancholy, grief for someone not yet born, not even yet partly formed.

Fortunately, a few days later Oge's hormone levels are back to normal. They get better than normal as the weeks go by.

The six-week ultrasound scan reveals a scratchy prototype of the human form: gourd-shaped head; rugby ball body; L-shaped legs like stylised clip art.

PART 5. SOLVING THE PANIC PARADOX?

1

It's wonderful when an event you're convinced will be terrifying turns out to be anything but. Within twenty minutes of Oge's injection with local anaesthetic and the nurses lifting up the bed sheets so we can't see the gore, baby Amara is plucked out of the womb and held aloft. She's beautiful. You wouldn't expect me to say otherwise. The whole procedure is disarmingly quick and straightforward. Now I understand why, earlier in the preparatory ward, there were a half dozen other couples awaiting C-section, all on the assurance it would happen today. The NHS have got this down to a fine – and efficient – art. We've been on the best conveyor belt ever.

It's a sign of the times that three nurses offer to take mobile snaps of our extremely new family. At just a few minutes old, Amara has been inducted into the all-knowing, all-seeing virtual network – soon enough she'll be susceptible to all the anxiety cues that the psychologists warn about. In the words of Jonathan Haidt, like other digital natives, she'll soon be 'exposed to ... cruelty and bullying because social media platforms incentivize and facilitate relational aggression'. As a girl, her 'openness and willingness to share emotions with other girls [will] espouse them to depression and other disorders'.

Let's park that for now, I say to myself, *and enjoy this moment.*

Back at the ward, I look down at this adorable, defenceless little blob. The imperative to keep her alive weighs me down like a suitcase full of Sumo wrestlers. One duff move could spell tragedy. Nothing I've done in my life has had higher stakes to it. As I look to Oge, who winces as she tries to express and latch Amara to her teat, the first person singular expands into the plural. *We* are responsible. But, going against my previous anti-white-coat syndrome when my anxiety has been lessened by knowing that expertise is at hand, in this case the *we* can't also encompass the doctors, nurses and state-of-the-art kit around us. I can't rid myself of the feeling that Oge and I are responsible for Amara, and no one else is. I don't like to admit this because it sounds like a sleight on the NHS, who have been and continue to be saintly towards us. But perhaps a primeval instinct is kicking in that predates the NHS. My genes are telling me we're still troglodytes who can rely only on our own wits and maybe some basic swaddling and a fire.

We feel more estranged from our cocoon every time an ambassador from a breastfeeding charity opens our curtains. The ambassador is blonde and bubbly like a kids' TV presenter. On the first visit she asks us through a grin if we're managing to breastfeed.

'I'm trying, O,' says Oge, still wincing. She doesn't look up from Amara, who has at least now connected with the teat. The usually unflappable Oge is anxious, I can tell, and anxiety can be infectious.

The ambassador talks of the need for a firm latch, for tummy-to-tummy positioning, for a hand to support the baby's head while she imbibes the good stuff.

On the next visit the ambassador explains all this again. She watches Oge do it properly and says, 'That's great.' She comes back to explain it ... again. The process is repeated another couple of times.

The problem is, each feed is never enough. As soon as Amara detaches from the breast, her little eyes screw into dots and her mouth bursts open to the size of a communion wafer and she screams like a siren whistle. If you've never heard your own child make such a bloodcurdling noise, which only gets worse as they struggle to catch their breath in order to make more of that noise, then count yourself lucky. While there are those who advocate controlled crying and the like, I – we – can't ignore our baby's wailing. The breast-muzzling tactic turns out to be unsustainable. By midnight, Oge is exhausted, and she places Amara into my hands quickly and smoothly like a rugby player making a pass. I hold her facing me, my left hand behind her head and my right on her bottom. She stares at me with her mother's glossy, coffee-bean-like eyes. Those eyes start to blink. That mouth widens. She's going to scream the ward down again. I have to think fast how to halt it.

If any incident will beget situational anxiety, this is it. I can feel my ticker drumming, lungs locking. I glance to Oge who's snoring away. She cannot be disturbed. I have to act.

As I watch Amara shaping up to go off again, I have the random thought that holding her this way is like gripping a musical instrument. That in turn gives me the idea to sing something. I can't recall any songs from my childhood save for an obscure ditty that goes, 'You can't put your muck in our dustbin, our dustbin, our dustbin/You can't put your muck in our dustbin, our dustbin's full.' Back into my head jumps a remark a nurse made earlier about babies enjoying gentle motion because it reminds them of the womb. I clamp Amara against my chest and stomp around the ward while serenading her with these stupid lyrics. To my amazement she nods off and stays that way. I pace around with her for five minutes, ten minutes, fifteen, singing this bloody song over and over again.

Though not the most epic expedition ever undertaken, Amara is travelling – sort of – and she's satisfied, apparently. My favourite travel writer, Bruce Chatwin, had a flamboyant if flawed theory that wanderlust was integral to human nature. He embraced nomadic peoples across the world, from the Australian Aborigines to the Bedouins, and pointed accusingly at the raft of social and psychic problems he felt were caused by 'settled society'. The impulse to roam manifests early in the baby's need to be rocked, Chatwin thought.

I try gently spinning Amara around so that I can hold her while she faces the same way as me. It works – I keep moving and she stays quiet. Having run out of songs I can remember, I hum a made-up tune and look at her face. It's neither tired nor alert, neither happy nor sad, just calm and accepting. It makes me think about the future. Now she's actually here with me, now that she's made it out of the womb and into the world, after all the odds against it, I can see a more positive destiny for her than the dystopian musings I had when she was just an idea, an aspiration. Yes, the world may be turning to shite but what if another baby represents an opportunity, however slim, to make the world a little less shitey? What if she can at least bring some joy as an artist or a musician or a writer? What if she can help or educate or inspire others? And so what if she doesn't do any of that but leads a fun and fulfilling life, enjoying love, friendship, food, travel and all the other stuff that the billions of sperm that never made it will never get to experience?

When we're discharged and return home, my sister-in-law gifts us what I distastefully call 'the electric chair'. It's a seat that jerks around in various directions while playing midi versions of 'Lord of the Dance' and 'Canon in D' that get so grating that I'm regularly tempted to hurl the contraption through the window – having removed my baby from it first, of course. The electric chair doesn't relax Amara. She still prefers being held by a human, walked around and being sung to – however badly. Oge suggests trading the electric chair in for a machine that can do this for us. I go down several internet rabbit holes looking for one and find only automated vacuum cleaners and primitive sex robots.

2

I learn more about patience in the paltry two weeks of my paternity leave than I have in 45 years. One reason is that no one in this situation can afford to be paralysed with anxiety. Instinct has a third way after flight and fight: *protect*. The forms of anxiety I've explored in this book so far are inward and self-centred. The fear has been all about *me*, much as I don't want it to be. Am *I* embarrassing myself? Am *I* going crazy? Am *I* dying? But feeding, burping, changing and cleaning a baby – having to do everything for it – necessarily puts the spotlight on her and off me. It's only natural to feel uneasy about all this, too, but it's not an unease that will overwhelm me because it *just can't*. If it does then my baby won't survive and I will have failed to propagate the species, from evolution's point of view. It may be a biological *and* social compulsion, as neglecting your child is, thankfully, a taboo in most cultures.

Over that fortnight, I suffer nothing more than the occasional pang of situational anxiety when, for instance, we realise that Amara won't fit in the shoddy car seat we've bought to ferry her to a doctor's appointment. At the hardest moments – the protracted screaming, the sleepless nights, the Herculean task of returning to and functioning at work – I retain my resolve. I don't panic.

That said, introducing Amara to the outside world, taking her on more ambitious journeys than up and down the hallway, brings fresh trials. While Oge takes a much-needed rest, I'll push the babe in the stroller around our neighbourhood and point out anything that might interest her eager, ever-searching eyes. A red postbox. A swooping seagull. A tomcat perching arrogantly on a shed roof like a dictator on a balcony above a brainwashed crowd. A bloke on a bike with insanely chunky tyres who almost flattens us because he can't be arsed to cycle on the road.

People often stop us and say, 'She's gorgeous, isn't she?' To which I reply, 'My preferred pronoun is *he*, but thank you anyway.' Now I'm a dad I reckon I can get away with such quips. Sometimes the compliments are soured by assumptions. A student type in Converse trainers and a Nirvana T-shirt – who could have time-travelled forward from my student days – asks if I'm Amara's grandfather. When I politely tell her absolutely bloody not, her entire body atrophies from embarrassment. After the third geriatric white woman asks if Amara is mine – perhaps folks who grew up on *The Black and White Minstrel Show* can't get their heads around mixed-race children – I declare with a plastic grin that no, I've abducted her. Fortunately, the police aren't waiting when we get home. None of these indiscretions affect Amara – oh, the boons of being pre-linguistic – so I can treat them with the contempt they deserve. So far as I'm triggered, I only have to deal with the spent bullet of mild annoyance rather than the point-blank headshot of deadly panic. That's because, again, it's not about me anymore, it's about her.

Another trial comes in the form of a friend's wedding. Oge and I have committed to taking not only young Amara but elderly Patricia, my mother-in-law. She's staying with us in keeping with an Igbo custom which compels a mother to support her daughter for the first couple of months of child-raising. Patricia isn't very mobile and needs a knee replacement. The question of why she didn't have the op before she came to help look after the baby is not worth a marriage-risking argument over. In the run-up to what will be Amara's most demanding adventure yet I don't feel anxiety so much as lethargic reluctance. I'll take this as progress. In the weeks running up to the event I have to sieve for whatever resolve I can find like a prospector who's come too late to the gold rush. I start fantasising about trains being cancelled and dignitaries dying – just how famous do you have to be for there to be a day of national mourning? – so we don't have to go through the tedious hassle of schlepping all that way with plaintive young and old relatives in tow.

Throughout the elaborate cortège of taxis and trains that we take from Portsmouth, Amara stays improbably cool. Oge dubs her 'the empress' for, beneath snazzy headgear that resembles the ceremonial turban of a maharaja, Amara's expression is at once content and supercilious. Most crucially for us she isn't screaming. Patricia is another story, though. Her limited mobility means taking elevators rather than even short flights of stairs and we almost miss one train due to her tardiness. Once aboard said train she informs us that she'd rather have stayed at home.

Unfortunately, we miss the exchange of vows due not only to Patricia's difficulties but my miscalculation of the time our final taxi will take to get across London.

'You *are* a travel writer, aren't you?' Oge snarls, as we make our way into the reception.

'There's a debate about that,' I reply. 'And besides, I'm knackered from being a dad.'

We all expect Amara to melt down from the louder, brighter new location. Au contraire – like an actress at the Oscars mobbed by paparazzi, she's besieged by friends and relatives, and smothered with kisses and more compliments about her beauty. In return she dispenses a couple of enigmatic smiles and noises approaching laughter. Afterwards, I check whether her head has grown too big for her to be comfortably returned to the car seat.

3

If the young are supposed to learn from the old, then the old can – and should – also learn from the young. Amara's wedding trip has been an object lesson in un-anxious travel. It's uber-impressive when you consider that, for someone who hasn't been in this world very long, this expedition would have been as new and startling as a grown-up conquering Kilimanjaro or landing on the moon. While of course travel anxiety is a complex phenomenon with many causes and effects, I can't help but feel like I, who has been travelling for thirty years, must raise my resilience game given what my daughter has achieved in three months.

I need all my resilience to clear the next hurdle in my post-fatherhood travel career. If going somewhere with Amara has been a success, I hope that going somewhere without her won't be a fiasco. I'm due to travel to Nepal as part of a university research project supporting women climate change activists and I'm not very optimistic about it after speaking to my friend Iain Overton about a tricky experience he had twenty years ago as a new father. I'll let him take up the story.

'When I was working as a BBC producer, I was told by my bosses that, if I wanted to stay in London, I would have to do the jobs that were given to me. I didn't have much agency in that process.

'My daughter was born around the time I was called into the office and told that I'd have to make a series about conflicts around the world. In the previous year, I'd been to a number of conflict zones so I was suffering from legacy trauma. I'd been shot at in Iraq, for instance, and I hadn't dealt with the emotions stemming from that. I was told I had to go and investigate the breakaway state of Somaliland.

'I spent around three weeks in the fug of a wonderful family unit and admiring my daughter's little hands and feet and every single little thing she did, as young parents do. My world was suddenly compressed into this small space inside which was just me, my daughter and her mother. I was shifted from this whirlwind of activity to Mogadishu, Somalia. There wasn't much in the way of pre-planning – we had two days to prep for our trip. The diktat we were given was: film everything, just never stop. This was a country about which there was very little coverage in the West. Before I'd left I'd spoken to a couple of academics about Somalia and Somaliland and the tensions between them. But there was no guidebook to Mogadishu.

'Before I knew it, I was on a connecting flight to Nairobi from London Heathrow and I remember walking down the gangway, every step another step away from my child and into a great unknown. I was convinced that each of those steps were towards my own death. I felt as though I was on a conveyor belt – if I turned around and went back to my family, I'd lose my job with the BBC. So I was forced to go travelling.

'The anxiety came out of mixed feelings about myself and what I was doing. Before I'd gone I'd been told repeatedly how lucky I was that I was being asked to do this and how brilliant an opportunity it was. But simultaneously, it was all wrapped up in this fear that, if I don't do it, my career will end overnight.

'Within forty-eight hours, we were in a barren field on the outskirts of Mogadishu with ten guys in the back of a pickup truck and a heavy machine gun on top. They were chewing *kat*, a local drug. It was boiling hot, fifty-odd degrees. A dead cow was in the middle of the road. There had been shootings the night before and I was conscious of two journalists who had gone there just before me and both been killed in the fighting. We were in a place of extreme tension.

'At the end of that first day, I shut the door of my hotel room. I felt like I was in a grave. I was in this whitewashed room that had no windows, which was boiling hot. Terror lurked outside. I was the opposite of where I wanted to be, which was lying next to my daughter on a bed. I missed that comfort.'

4

My mission in Nepal isn't nearly as stressful as Iain's was in Somalia. That doesn't mean it goes smoothly. On the second day I come down with a stomach infection. I'll spare you the details, but I spend so much time in a toilet cubicle that when people ask me now what Nepal is like all I can say is, 'They have quite a range of loo roll holders.' When I'm not recycling the little food and drink I can get down my top end, I'm lying in bed pining for my wife and baby. This kind of homesickness is new to me and reflects the changes I've undergone relatively late in life: marriage and fatherhood. The melancholy of missing loved ones is no fun, but it's better than anxiety. Looking at pictures of Amara and allowing myself to weep over them seems like a natural process and I feel better at the end of it. If the theory I mentioned in the intro to this book is correct, blocking out such emotions might have provoked the anxiety beast.

When my colleagues invite me on a hike around the Himalayan foothills, I determine that it's not worth having to find a firethorn bush to crap behind every twenty minutes. I stay in my room where the latrine is accessible. It's regrettable, it's annoying, it's as boring as a Coldplay gig at a trainspotters' convention ... but I'll take it any day over low- to mid-level anxiety and certainly over agitation, that inability to stay mentally and physically still. After all the squits I don't have the energy to be restless anyway.

The ante ups on my last day in Kathmandu. Tamsin, the professor leading the research trip, wants me to see a doctor before I fly home, just to be safe. It's a sweet, protective gesture. But I'm scared that I won't make it far down the road without needing to drop yet more friends off at the pool – and that will not end happily if I'm perched on the back of a Yamaha scooter. Tamsin says we can call a doctor out.

'It's alright, I've only got the shits,' I protest.

An hour later, two paramedics knock on my hotel room door. They have stethoscopes, blood pressure cuffs and other kit dangling over their shoulders like soldiers with ammo belts. One of them asks me to stick out my tongue. 'I think you're dehydrated, sir.'

'I'll drink more water.'

'We prefer you to come to the hospital, sir.'

Tamsin arrives and concurs.

I make a prayer steeple with my hands. 'Can I still fly home tomorrow and see my baby? Please?'

We go out to the front of the hotel where a full-sized ambulance is parked, not one of these jumped-up saloon cars they have in the UK now. A paramedic tells me to sit on a stretcher. He wheels me inside the ambulance. I can feel my cheeks going nuclear with embarrassment. Not for the first time, I fret about having deprived someone who genuinely needs this VIP treatment. Tamsin climbs into the front next to the driver, who turns the siren on.

'I've only got the shits,' I say again as we start driving.

Tamsin bursts out laughing.

It is a mere eight minutes' drive to the hospital. Given the traffic, it would have been quicker to have walked – or been wheeled in a stretcher. At the hospital I'm helped out of the stretcher, ushered into a ward, prodded, patted, cuffed and pricked. 'I've only got the shits,' I say once more.

'Better to take precautions, sir,' says a female Indian doctor. 'If you are dehydrated and sepsis happens then you will be in a great deal of trouble.'

A cynical voice somewhere inside me – my anti-Jiminy Cricket, if you like – floats the idea that a Global Southern private hospital gives patients such close attention so that it can maximise the money it can claim back from a Global

Northern insurance company. I stand corrected when a blood test reveals that my liver enzymes are hazardously high. That gets me hooked up to a couple of drips.

My watch beeps for 8pm. 'Can I still catch my morning flight?'

'We should keep you in overnight,' says the doctor.

I want Tamsin to tell me that we can't re-book the flight or add another day's stay at the hotel, or find some other reason for me *having* to leave tomorrow. But she's far too kind and efficient – within an hour she's sorted all that out with the insurance company.

I'm shown into my private room in the hospital. With its flatscreen TV, sparkling ensuite facilities and room service it's only marginally less salubrious than my hotel. But none of that makes the video call to Oge any easier.

'They say it's too risky for me to travel yet. It wouldn't be clever to get sepsis on the plane.'

Oge isn't convinced. 'But it is only diarrhoea, *abi*?'

She moves her camera down to Amara's face, which is half-hidden by the pink blanket she's pulled over herself. She's changed so much in the week I've been away. She has more hair, which has gathered of its own volition into a samurai-like topknot. She's smiling more, with fuller lips and even more beguiling eyes. Smile more – there's another lesson to be learned from someone 45 years my junior.

I manage a quick hello and a blown kiss before the lump in my throat grows too big and I have to end the call. I don't want my loved ones to know that I'm miserable. I also have this more irrational dread that, if they see me upset, they'll be able to read my mind and figure out what's making me so. They'll see that I'm scared that Amara won't recognise me by the time I get home and that I'm feeling ever more guilty about having left Oge to look after our demanding baby. To be fair, I wouldn't have gone at all if Oge hadn't assured me that she'd be fine with her mum's support, but that doesn't console me now as I cry myself to sleep – or the best sleep one can have when lashed to various machines that beep, flash and gurgle all night.

The next morning I feel better in every way. The drips have done their job. I'm rehydrated and less infected. I'm getting out of here today and I'll be home with my family tomorrow. I'm also buoyed by reminding myself of my job here, even though my illness has diverted me from it. I'm travelling ethically and respectfully, for a good cause: to support women who are standing against gender-based violence and state repression, and for their reproductive and labour rights. My part in this is microscopically small, but it's still a part.

Iain has a similar feeling about why he travels these days. 'There is a sense of profound purpose for capturing the suffering of others. I've learned what *not* to do from my early career when I'd be in an all-white film crew turning up in a country to mock its culture. I wouldn't make those kinds of films now. In my work now, I'm challenging imperialism and exposing abuses.'

While I wait for the discharge paperwork, I reflect on my sadness last night. It was different – and better – than anxiety because it was comprehensible. It happened for a reason. It was the logical outcome of loneliness and separation. It didn't ambush me from nowhere. It didn't debilitate me, as anxiety will.

I return to my hotel. I'm on the mend and I mustn't sabotage myself. I eat a light meal. I don't go out and drink alcohol, despite a tempting invitation to join another colleague and their Nepali friends at a chichi restaurant. I maintain that discipline for the trip home the next day and am rewarded with a stable gut and a relaxing flight.

5

The Nepal trip has taught me about perspective, about accepting things I can't control. Learning in hospital that I'd be 24 hours late back to the bosom of my family was an emotional carpet bombing, but I know that the delay saved me from dashing in and out of aeroplane toilets and wrecking my liver and chuff knows what else.

During a routine visit, a midwife notices Amara is tongue-tied and we get her what they call 'the snip'. At around that same time an amiable young GP breaks with NHS dogma to tell Oge that there's no shame in supplementing breast milk with formula. 'Breastfeeding comes in and out of fashion,' he says. Now that Amara's feeding better she has longer periods of being content *not* to roam. She'll lie on her back in her cot, still scanning the room with intense curiosity, while I read. Sometimes I'll read out loud to her from a children's book which keeps her pacified. When she gets bored of that or has fallen asleep at last, I'll read to myself, which distracts me from sleep deprivation and worries that have built up over the day.

My friend, the novelist and academic Victoria Leslie, is a big fan of reading for wellbeing. Her travels have taken her to remote parts like Shetland, and she's staved off loneliness and anxiety by 'stocking up on books'. In busier environments such as London Underground trains when there's a risk of catastrophising, 'I read and it occupies my mind,' she tells me. 'It puts things into perspective. You relate to a character in a story or what a writer is trying to achieve with that story. It just makes things more manageable. You don't feel quite so alone in the moment.'

I wouldn't be so bold as to say fatherhood has cured my anxiety, but since Amara came along I haven't had a critical episode like the ones described in this book. Focusing on someone else's welfare over your own has helped, as mentioned, for catching planes and meeting new people in foreign places seem so trivial as to be fictional, as to have never happened, when compared to being responsible for a child growing up healthy and happy.

Fatherhood has also obliged me to be a more responsible human being. If trying to get a baby off to sleep at 3am is hard enough sober, it's torture when you're doing it after a few pints and Hypnos is beckoning you to the land of dreams. I confess that I did once fall asleep for a few minutes sitting upright with Amara still cradled in my arms. I was sober when I did that, but if I hadn't been I might have dropped her – or worse. The Crown Office and Procurator Fiscal Service (COPFS) found that almost a third of infant deaths in Scotland in 2023 were a result of babies co-sleeping with parents who were intoxicated on drink and/or drugs.

So not only has my newfound moderation made my daughter safer, it's decreased my dangerous spirals of drinking to feel better one day, only to be stricken with hangxiety the next, which means getting back on the sauce to fight off the hangxiety, which only worsens things the following day and so on.

Another anxiety trap that I find easier to dodge – but that the earlier me would have walked right into – is the one laid by jobsworths. When you become a parent, you're introduced to a whole new army of them in hospitals, GP surgeries, pharmacies, registry offices and so on. This isn't to say that there aren't many kind-hearted and competent employees of these institutions, but when I meet a Kafkaesque Karen or Kevin, I stay chill and follow my friend the travel writer Shafik Meghji's advice: 'These people are often not very well paid. A lot of pressure is on them. If you get into a tricky or perilous situation with them you cannot necessarily empathise, but you can try and put yourself into the shoes of that person on the other side of the desk, even if they're being a pain in the neck for no apparent reason. You can try and understand what their potential motivations are. That might suggest a route out of the situation.' I've learned not to take the bait. If someone wants to lord it over you for five minutes, let them do it. As long as you get your prescription or your carton of formula.

I've learned that I can't live a life completely void of anxiety. On this I'm with those writers and philosophers mentioned at the start of this book. A fear-free existence is not only unrealistic but undesirable, for all the psychoanalytical reasons stated above: there's no meaning without struggle; no journey without obstacles; no story without conflict. It's about managing your life so that anxiety doesn't ruin it. About finding strategies to nip the fear in the bud as and when it starts to freak you out. About avoiding longer-term bad habits from set-tos with pencil-pushers to necking substances for brief relief. About doing your bit as a citizen and as an activist to try to change our social contract that condemns so many to anxiety-inducing work conditions and economic situations.

For now, I'm just glad to not be *such* an anxious traveller – or anxious person generally.

SOURCES

Achebe, C. (2020) *No Longer at Ease*. Dead Authors' Society.

Adichie, C.N. (2017). *Purple Hibiscus*. Fourth Estate.

Allen, W. (1975). *Death: A Comedy in One Act*. Samuel French, Inc.

Amos, S. (Director). (2004). *Doug Stanhope: Deadbeat Hero*. Best Medicine.

Augé, M. (2009). *Non-places: Introduction to an Anthropology of Supermodernity*. Verso.

Bierce, A. (2001). *The Enlarged Devil's Dictionary*. Penguin Classics.

Bulosan, C. (2022; 1946). *America is in the Heart*. Penguin Vitae.

Campbell, J. (2012). *The Hero With a Thousand Faces*. New World Library.

Capote, T. (2000; 1958). *Breakfast at Tiffany's*. Penguin Classics.

Carroll, E. J. (1993). *Hunter: The Strange and Savage Life of Hunter S. Thompson*. Dutton.

Chatwin, B. (1997; 1987). *The Songlines*. Pan Macmillan.

Chatzichristodoulou, M., Zerihan R. & Jefferies J. (Eds.). (2012). *Interfaces of Performance*. Ashgate Publishing Ltd.

Chrisafis, A. (2006, December 20). Paris Syndrome' strikes Japanese. *BBC News*. news.bbc.co.uk/1/hi/6197921.stm

Csikszentmihalyi, M. (2008). *Flow: The Psychology of Optimal Experience*. HarperPerennial.

Curran, A. (2024, January 26). Safety plea over co-sleeping baby death figures. *BBC News*. https://www.bbc.co.uk/news/uk-scotland-68101937?utm_source=chatgpt.com

Boorman, J. (Director). (1972). *Deliverance*. Warner Bros.

Correspondent. (2003, February 5). 'My holidays in the Axis of Evil'. *BBC News*. http://news.bbc.co.uk/1/hi/programmes/correspondent/2728249.stm

De Botton, A. (2002). *The Art of Travel*. Pantheon Books.

Ellard, C. (2015). *Places of the Heart: The Psychogeography of Everyday Life*. Bellevue Literary Press.

Freeman, D., & Freeman J. (2012). *Anxiety: A Very Short Introduction*. Oxford University Press.

Freud, S. (2010; 1930). *Civilization and its Discontents*. W. W. Norton & Company.

Freud, S. (2004; 1913). *Totem and Taboo*. Routledge Classics.

Goldhagen, D. (1997). *Hitler's Willing Executioners: Ordinary Germans and the Holocaust*. Abacus.

Haidt, J. (2024). *The Anxious Generation: How the Great Rewiring of Childhood Is Causing an Epidemic of Mental Illness*. Penguin.

Hamilton-Paterson, J. (1987). *Playing with Water: Alone on a Philippine Island*. Macmillan.

Harrison, M. J. (2023). *Wish I Was Here: An Anti-Memoir*. Serpent's Tail.

Hilberg, R. (2003). *The Destruction of the European Jews*. Yale University Press.

Hitchens, C. (2010, June 28). The Narcissism of the Small Difference. *Slate.* https://slate.com/news-and-politics/2010/06/in-ethno-national-conflicts-it-really-is-the-little-things-that-tick-people-off.html

Hooper, T. (Director). (1974). *The Texas Chainsaw Massacre.* Bryanston Distributing Company.

Huffington, A. (2011). *Third World America: How Our Politicians Are Abandoning the Ordinary Citizen.* Collins.

Hutton, B.G. (Director). (1970). *Kelly's Heroes.* Katzka-Loeb Productions, Avala Film, The Warriors Company.

IQ Air. (2022). 2022 World Air Quality Report. https://www.iqair.com/newsroom/world-air-quality-report-press-release-2022?srsltid=AfmBOoqyGV_koZxqutur2pMoW-G3NJg8mtD30kAqGOWItTYzDyFVAeELc

James, O. (2008). *The Selfish Capitalist: Origins of Affluenza.* Vermilion.

Jeffers, S. (2007). *Feel the Fear and Do It Anyway.* Vermilion.

Jones, C.M., Scholes, L., Johnson, D., Katsikitis, M., & Carras, M.C. (2014). Gaming well: links between videogames and flourishing mental health. *Frontiers in Psychology, 31(5)*, 1-8. doi: 10.3389/fpsyg.2014.00260

Kafka, F. (2009; 1926). *The Castle.* Oxford University Press.

Kafka, F. (2022; 1915). *Metamorphosis.* Penguin Classics.

Kafka, F. (2021; 1925). *The Trial.* Legend Classics.

Kaufman, D. (2013, April 17). Should Selena Gomez apologize for wearing a bindi at the MTV Movie Awards? *Today.* http://today.com/popculture/selena-gomez-causes-controversy-wearing-bindi-mtv-movie-awards-i533548

King, Stephen. (2012; 1981). *Danse Macabre.* Hodder Paperbacks.

Lacan, J. (2007). *Écrits – The First Complete Edition in English* (B. Fink, Trans.). W. W. Norton & Company.

Lang, P. J. (1968). Fear reduction and fear behavior: Problems in treating a construct. In J. M. Shlien (Ed.), *Research in psychotherapy* (pp. 90–102). American Psychological Association. https://doi.org/10.1037/10546-004

Manson, M. (2016). *The Subtle Art of Not Giving a F*ck: A Counterintuitive Approach to Living a Good Life.* Harper.

McGowan, T. (2013). *Enjoying What We Don't Have: The Political Project of Psychoanalysis.* University of Nebraska Press.

March, B. (2018, July 17). Kim Kardashian defends her decision to wear cornrows. *Harper's Bazaar.* https://www.harpersbazaar.com/uk/beauty/hair/a22194079/kim-kardashian-defends-her-decision-to-wear-cornrows/

Mental Health Foundation. (2020). *Tackling social inequalities to reduce mental health problems: How everyone can flourish equally.* MHF-tackling-inequalities-report.pdf

Miller, S. (2009). *Delhi: Adventures in a Megacity*. Vintage.

Mourgue, G. (Director). (2020). *Amazing Hotels: Life Beyond the Lobby.* London: BBC.

Nashawaty, C. (2012, February 17). The Jerusalem Syndrome: Why Some Religious Tourists Believe They Are the Messiah. *Wired.* www.wired.com/2012/02/ff-jerusalemsyndrome/

Nietzsche, F. (1990). *Twilight of the Idols and The Anti-Christ.* Penguin Classics.

Orwell, G. (2021). *Nineteen Eighty-Four.* Penguin Classics.

Penman, D. and Williams. (2011). *Mindfulness: Finding Peace in a Frantic World*. Piatkus Books.

Proust, Marcel. (2001; 1913–1927). *In Search of Lost Time Box Set*. Everyman.

Rosca, N. (2007). *State of War*. Anvil Publishing.

Robinson, B. (Director). (1987). *Withnail & I*. Handmade Films.

Rushdie, S. (1998; 1988). *The Satanic Verses*. Vintage.

Sachdev, P. (1995). The development of the concept of akathisia: a historical overview. *Schizophrenia Research, 16*, 33-45. https://doi.org/10.1016/0920-9964(94)00058-G

Sartre, J-P. (1982; 1938). *Nausea*. Penguin Modern Classics.

Sartre, J-P. (2007; 1946). *Existentialism and Humanism*. Methuen Publishing Ltd.

Scott, P. (1981). *The Raj Quartet*. Guild.

Shakespeare, W. (1998). Hamlet. Edited by G.R. Hibbard. Oxford University Press.

Shore, D. (Creator). (2004-2012). *House*. [TV Programme]. New York: Heel and Toe Films, Shore Z Productions, Bad Hat Harry Productions, Universal Television.

Sykes, T. (2021). *Ivory Coast 2nd Edition*. Bradt.

Tarrog, J. (Director). (2018). *Goyo: The Boy General*. TBA Studios, Artikulo Uno Productions, Globe Studios.

Terrell, R. (1988). *West African Interlude*. Michael Russell Publishing Ltd.

Vogel, J. (2016, October 18). #105 Debate Lawrence Krauss vs Peter Rollins New Religions vs New Atheism 2013 [Video]. YouTube. URL

Vylenz, D. & Winkler, M. (Director). (2003). *The Mindscape of Alan Moore*. Shadowsnake Films.

The Wachowskis. (Directors). (1999). *The Matrix*. Warner Bros.

The Week Staff. (2022, June 17). The Shipping Forecast: is this much-loved British institution reaching the end of the road? *The Week*. theweek.com/from-the-magazine/957102/shipping-forecast-reaching-end-of-road

White, T.H. (2015). *The Goshawk*. W&N.

Wilde, O. (2000). *The Complete Letters*. (Holland, M. & Hart-Davis, R., Eds.). Fourth Estate.

Wolfe, T. (199). *This Boy's Life*. Bloomsbury.

Woolf, V. (2020; 1925). *Mrs Dalloway.* Penguin Modern Classics.

Xu, Y. (2018, December 1). Dolce & Gabbana Ad (With Chopsticks) Provokes Public Outrage in China. *NPR*. http://npr.org/sections/goatsandsoda/2018/12/01/671891818/dolce-gabbana-ad-with-chopsticks-provokes-public-outrage-in-china

Žižek, S. (2006). *How to Read Lacan.* Granta.

Žižek, S. (2008; 1989). *The Sublime Object of Ideology.* Verso.

ACKNOWLEDGEMENTS

Mammoth thanks to a number of fine people who read drafts of this book, gave me good pointers for it and/or helped and supported me in other vital ways. They include Ben Aitken, Ann Bajo, Karl Bell, Ellen Conlon, Stephen Harper, Sue Harper, Victoria Leslie, Shafik Meghji, Oge Okonkwo, Iain Overton, Matt Parsons, Connor Stait, Will Sutton, Lucy Sykes and Paul Valentine. An extra special bumper thank you to my patient and perspicacious editor Steve Burdett.